FEB 03 2017

P9-DNI-386

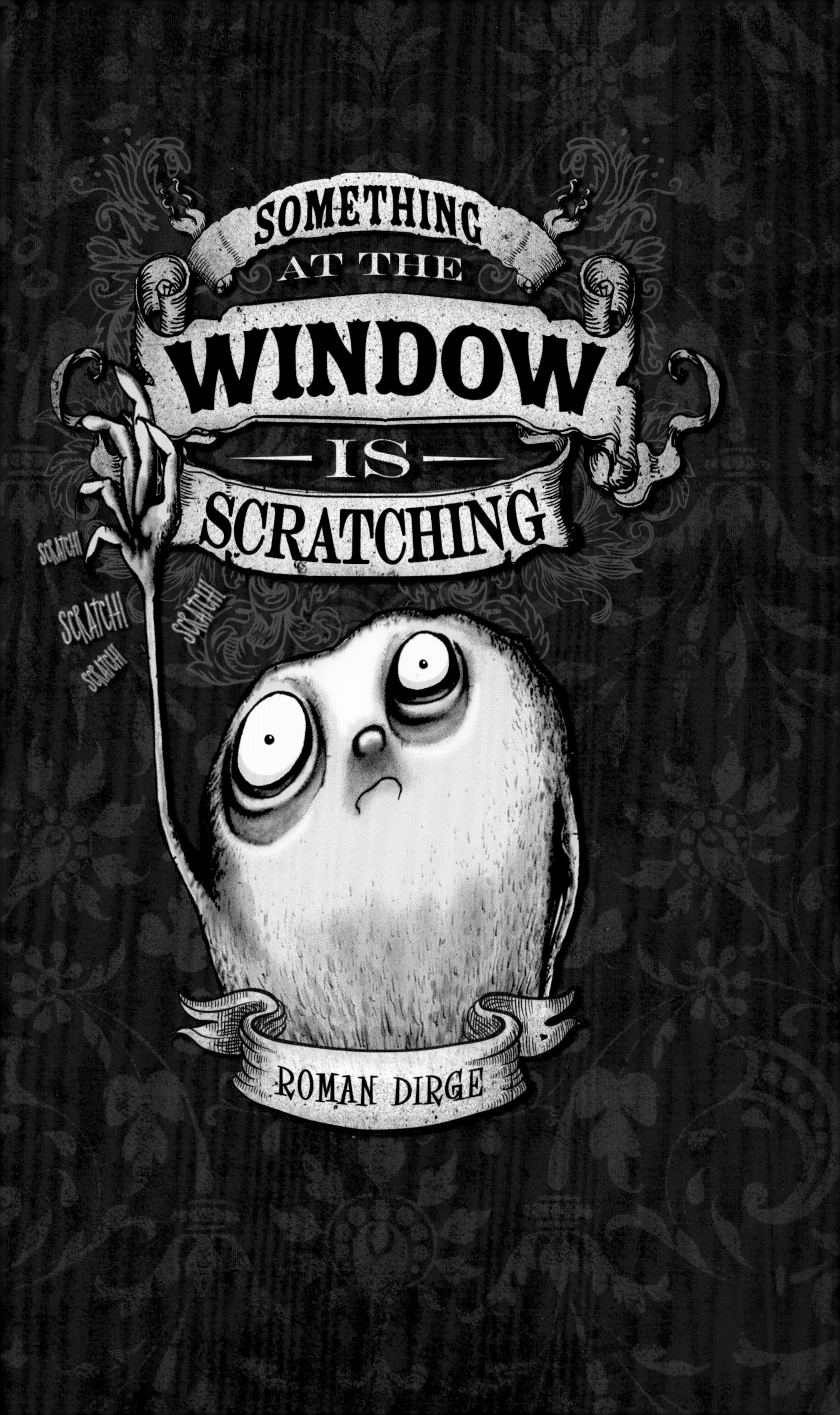
SOMETHING
AT THE
WINDOW
IS
SCRATCHING
SCRATCH!
SCRATCH!
SCRATCH
SCRATCH!
ROMAN DIRGE

SOMETHING AT THE WINDOW IS SCRATCHING

SCRATCH! SCRATCH! SCRATCH! SCRATCH!

ROMAN DIRGE

WRITTEN, DRAWN AND COLORED
BY ROMAN DIRGE

Titan Comics

SOMETHING AT THE WINDOW IS SCRATCHING
ISBN: 9781782763499

Published by Titan Comics, a division of Titan Publishing Group Ltd.,
144 Southwark St., London, SE1 0UP

This edition first published: September 2015

10 9 8 7 6 5 4 3 2 1

Something at the Window is Scratching is ™ & © 2015 Roman Dirge. All rights reserved. All
characters, events and institutions depicted herein and their distinctive likenesses thereof are
trademark of Roman Dirge.

No part of this publication may be reproduced, stored in a retrieval system, or transmitted, in
any form or by any means, without the prior written permission of the publisher. Any similarity
between any of the names, characters, persons, events and/or institutions in this publication
to actual names, characters, and persons, whether living or dead (except for satirical purposes)
and/or institutions are unintended and purely coincidental. TCN811

A CIP catalogue record for this title is available from the British Library.

Printed in China.

Something at the Window is Scratching was first published in the USA and Canada in 1998
by Slave Labor Graphics.

Contents

DEDICATED TO BOMB AND DAD

"This stuff just comes to you, huh?"
- My Dad.

Foreword

Think back. No, farther back than that. No, even farther than that. NO, are you...
Look, if you're not even going to try, then just forget it, okay? I hate you, I'm leaving.
Wait, let's try again, yes? Do you remember being small? Can you remember being a
disturbed little child? It's not as strange as it sounds to refer to kids, the proper ones
anyhow, as disturbed. Nothing's as strange as it sounds.

We expect so much from people by the time they have "grown up", so much stability
and too much... adulthood. You put a child's soul, symbol of purity, innocence and hope,
into a grownup's body, and you would have what Earthling society would call a lunatic.
The world would lock them away and wonder what went wrong with this unfortunate
person, while forever lamenting their own loss of the very qualities they interpret as
improper in the prisoner. Now I know what you're thinking, you're thinking, "So,
exactly HOW do you extract a child's soul from its body? And by what device do you
insert it into the body of a grownup? And what happened to the grownup's soul seeing
as how the body is empty when it receives the child's soul? Or is it NOT empty, but just
pushed back to make room for the child's soul, just stuffed back in the darkest reaches
of the body (perhaps the large intestine) screaming, SCREAMING to be released! Does
anybody hear the screaming? I'm scared." Well the answer is simple.

But I won't get into that.

It's a lovely thing, and an evil pain in the ass, to be the proud owner of such a soul.
Lovely, because things like this book make sense, and provoke a smile, a distant sense
of warmth in knowing that other brains are churning out the same beautiful nonsense
that actually touches something in you retained from when you were so much smaller.
Smaller and not a prisoner of expectation. It's a painful thing because you can see other
people losing these qualities as they grow with you. You can watch as they shed off
childhood like a skin they feel no longer suits them, emerging from this metamorphosis
as a beautifully majestic specimen of the mundane.

These miserable clothed monkeys aren't the prisoners though, as a prison needs to
contain something alive, something that knows there is more out there to be had.

Okay, I'm going to interrupt myself here and tell you that even I don't know where the hell I'm going with this thing. I'm not sure if it was supposed to be about how losing ones own ability to love the absurd is a horrible thing, or if I was trying to divulge the secrets to some ghoulish government plan to rip the souls from children so that they could learn more about that sort of thing. All I really know now is that kids have a quality about them that lets them be insane, and gives them a playful lunacy that, quite simply, kicks ass. To successfully hold on to that quality and add it to things learned while and upon growing up is something akin to a super weapon against reality. To be able to revel in disgusting tales, and stories about monsters, and pear-headed mutants whose friends get eaten by birds. To crack smiles, and laugh, and then honestly wonder how his bread-headed friend could have made it this long without having been eaten by birds longer ago.

I remember hearing stories like Red Riding Hood, and thinking with such focus on how it must have felt to be inside that wolf's stomach, and what it would have smelled like. I would try to imagine where the monsters in all of these classic stories came from, and how they lived before the stories began. Sometimes it's the lack of details that make the story so everlasting. And it's the same here, in Roman Dirge's little book, as I ask myself, "What the hell is up with the sandman? I mean he can't fly? What's his problem that he actually steps into a bear trap?" I imagine he was distracted by something, and just had a lapse of attention. Also, his little son's ass freaks me out. These little details that are no more but implied, save perhaps for that eerie little butt-thing, are what make stories like these stick in my mind, and the minds of all the other kids out there who find they're alive in a world of people who grew up and lost that special something, who grew up to be dead.

Okay, this thing ended up sounding so much more dreary than I had intended, but I got a semblance of a point across (not an easy task at times), and I think that point is clear to anyone who was actually paying attention:

Children are criminally insane and must be destroyed.

Jhonen Vasquez
Comic book writer, cartoonist, animator and creator of Nickelodeon's tInvader Zim.

THE COO COO LADY

There once was a lady
who loved her coo coo.
She sat in bed waiting –
that's all she would do.
Anxiously waiting
for that bird to appear,
knowing that soon
the time would be near.

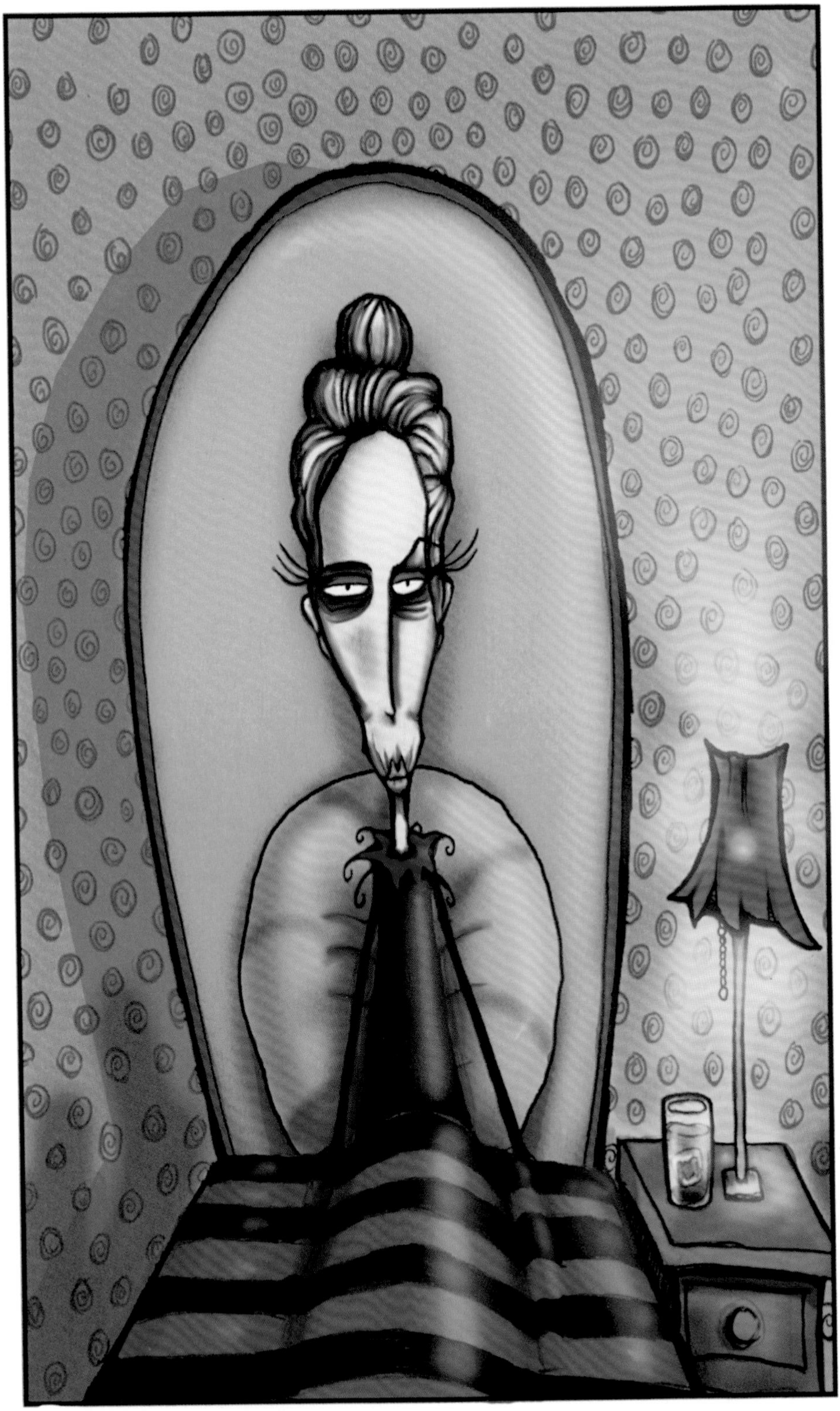

Twice a day at twelve
the bird would come out.
"I love you dear birdie!"
the coo coo lady
would shout.

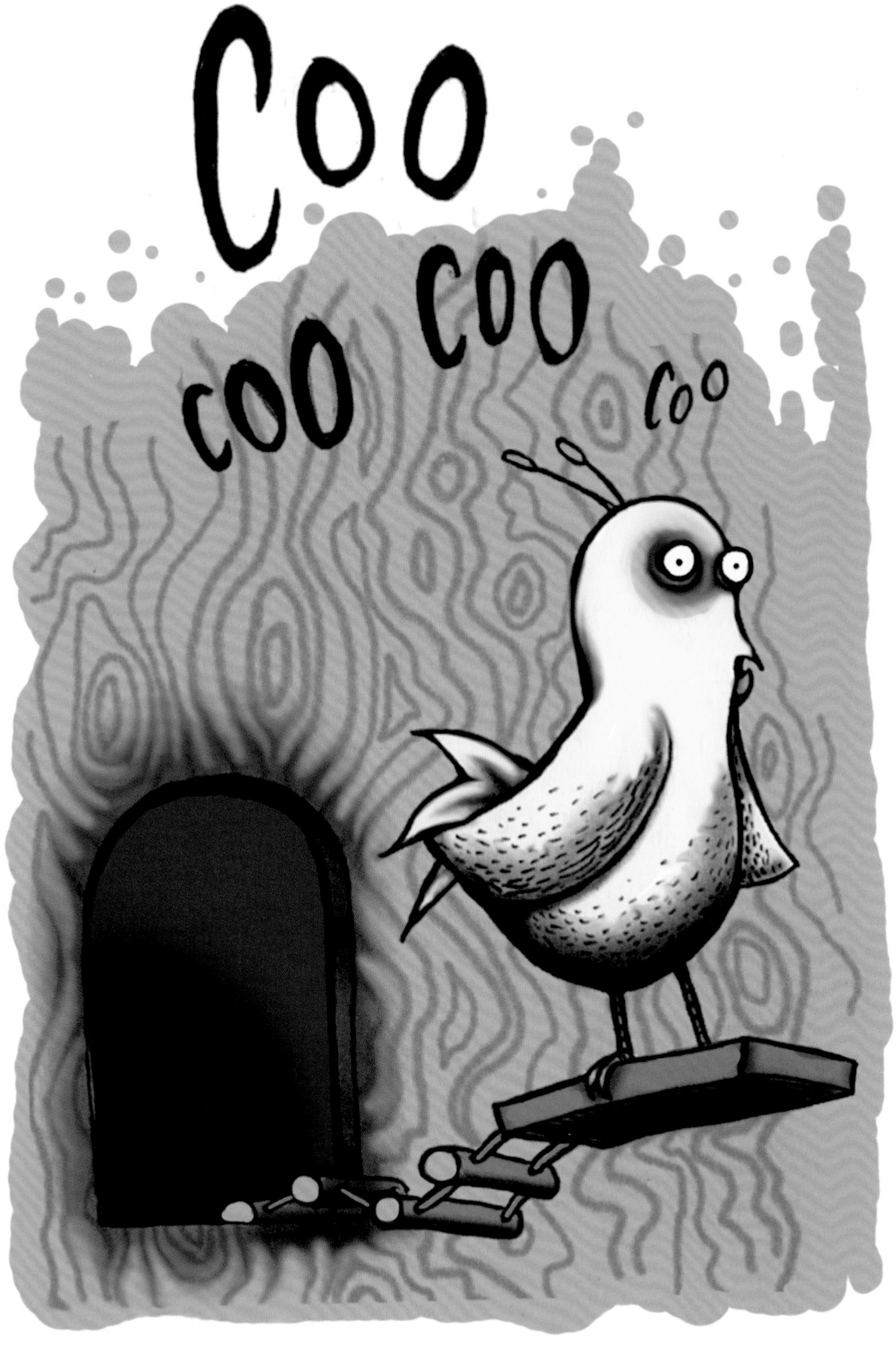

COO
COO COO
COO

After 70 years
of coo coo-ing
the bird would

coo coo no more.
Horrified –
the coo coo lady lost
all that she had lived for.

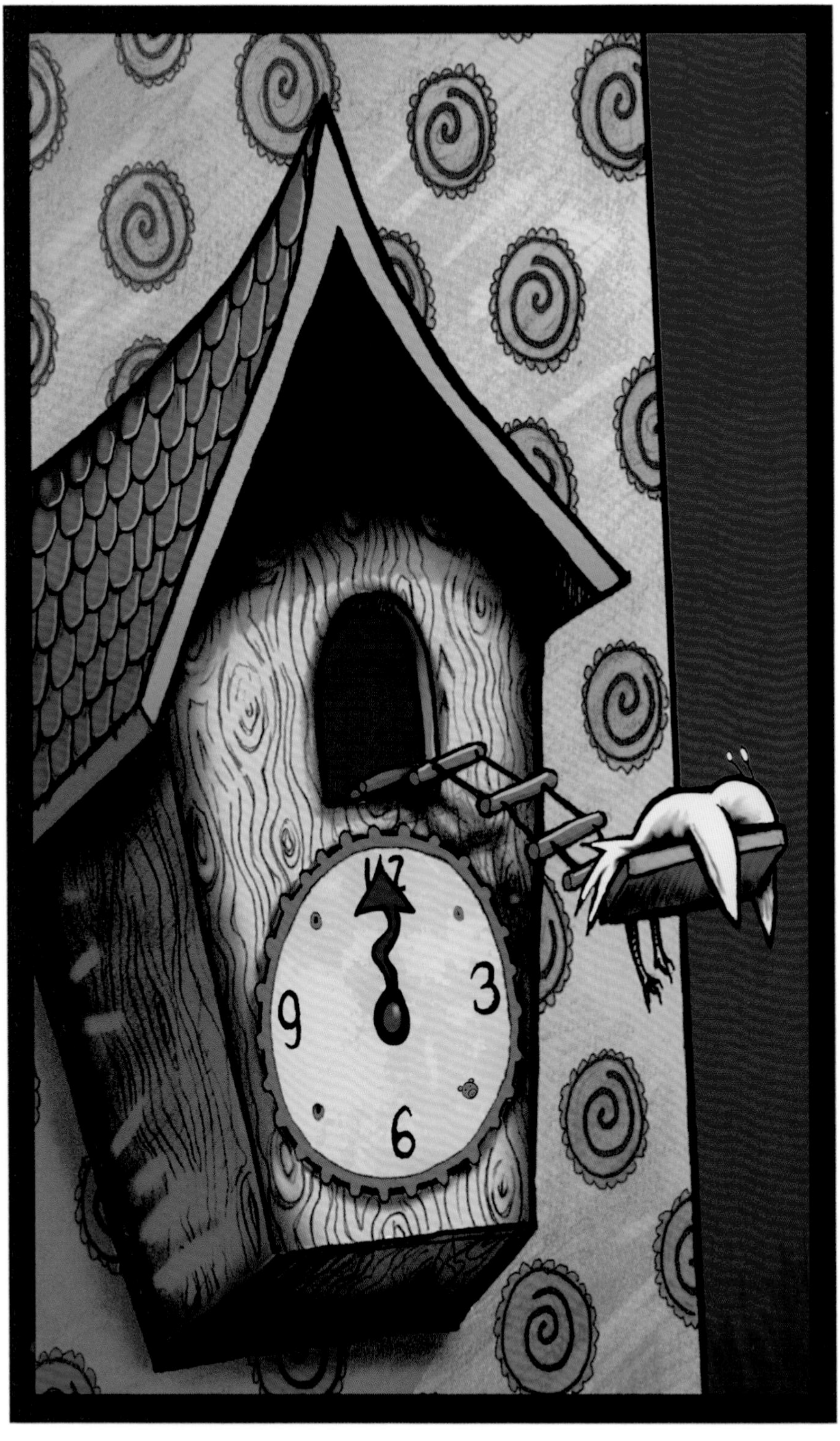

Quickly,
the coo coo lady fell over –
dead from a broken heart.
She and her birdie
left this world
only six seconds apart.

CRITTER PIE

A little horror,
A scream, a cry...
That's how you make a critter pie.
They beg.
They plead.
They try to run.
This makes cooking so much fun.
Four to five critters would be nice.
The "big-boned" ones just add spice.
Everything must someday die –
might as well make a critter pie.

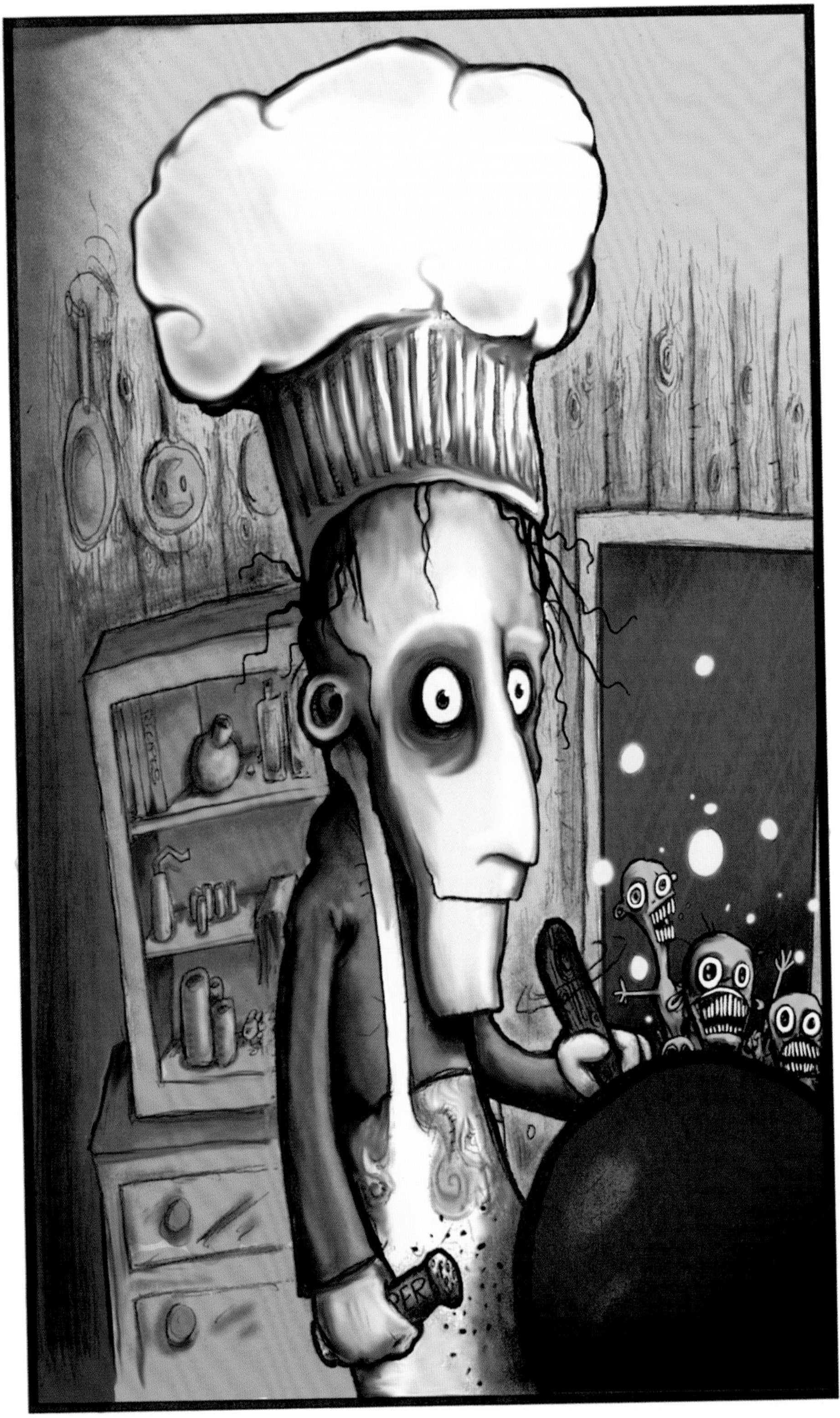

THE SIDEWAYS MAN

Long ago lived a vampire
whose body was crooked
on just one side.
He liked to take pictures
of all his victims
as they died.

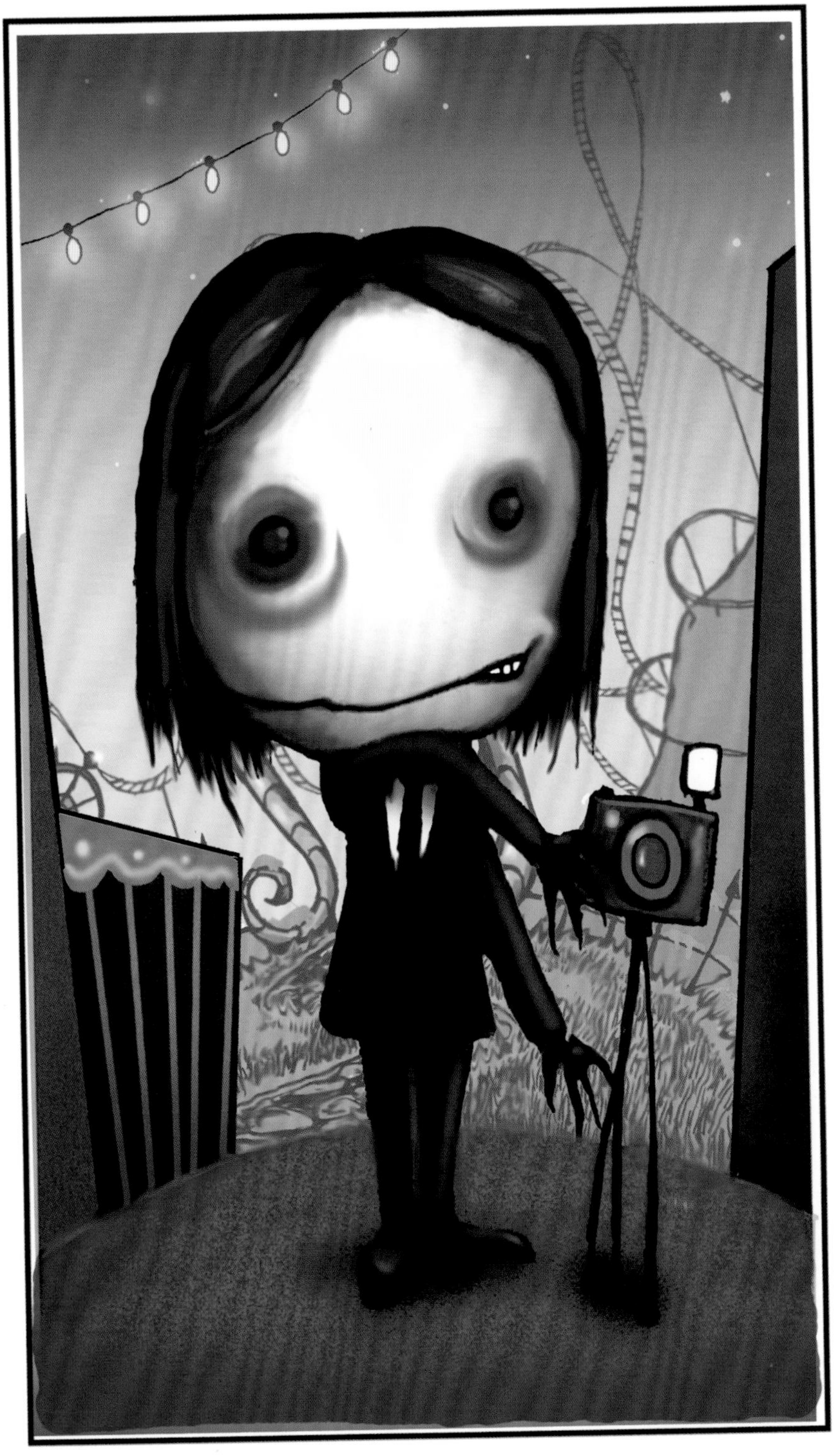

He toured with a carnival
that traveled coast to coast,
bragging to his vampire friends
that he had killed the most.

The Sideways Man heard a rumor
that there was another blood drinker in town.
So he went on a search,
destined to have
a vampire showdown.

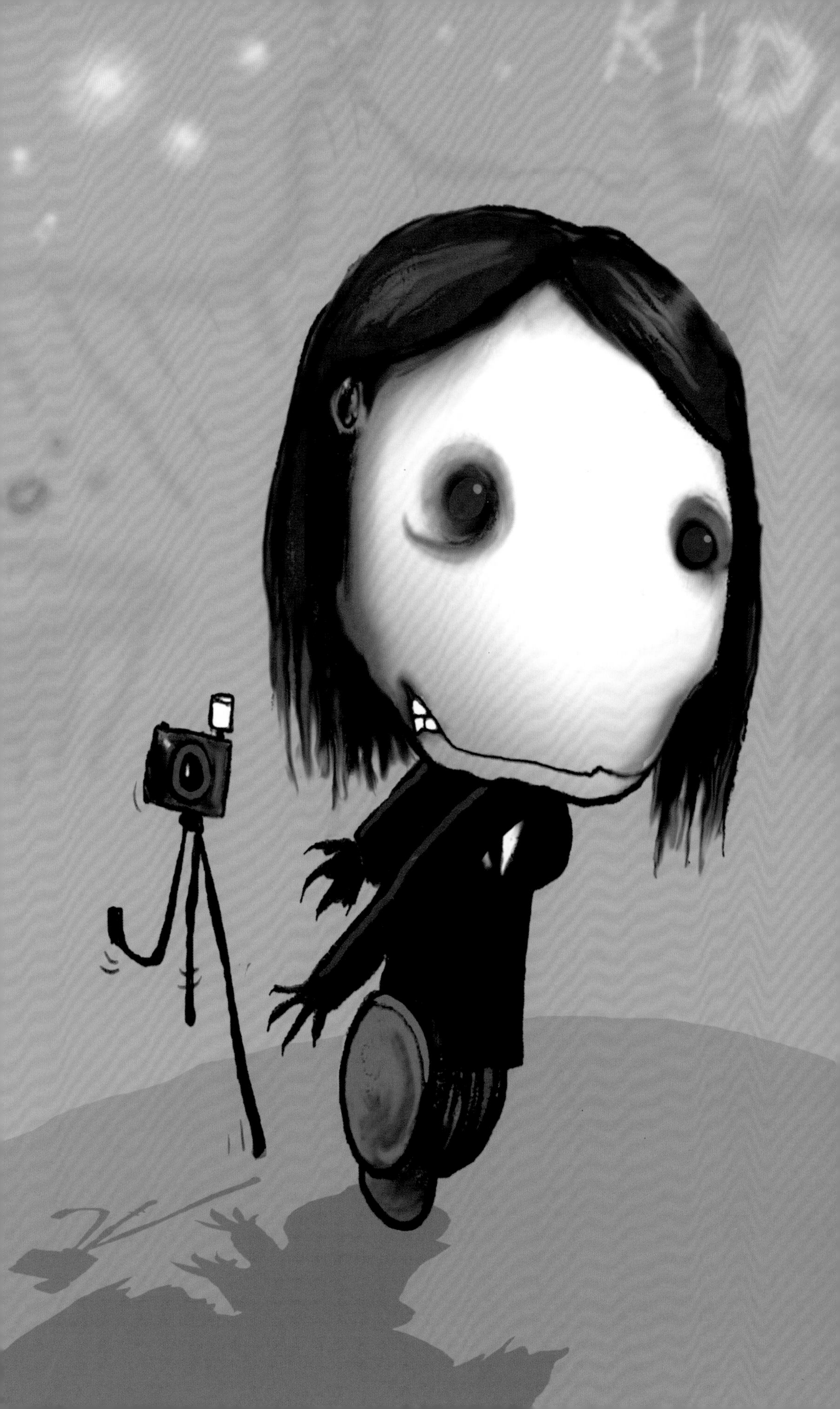

It didn't take long
to find the foe that he sought.
He expected many things,
but this he did not.
Walking his direction
in the nite dim,
The Sideways Man's
long lost brother Ragamuffin
now stood before him.

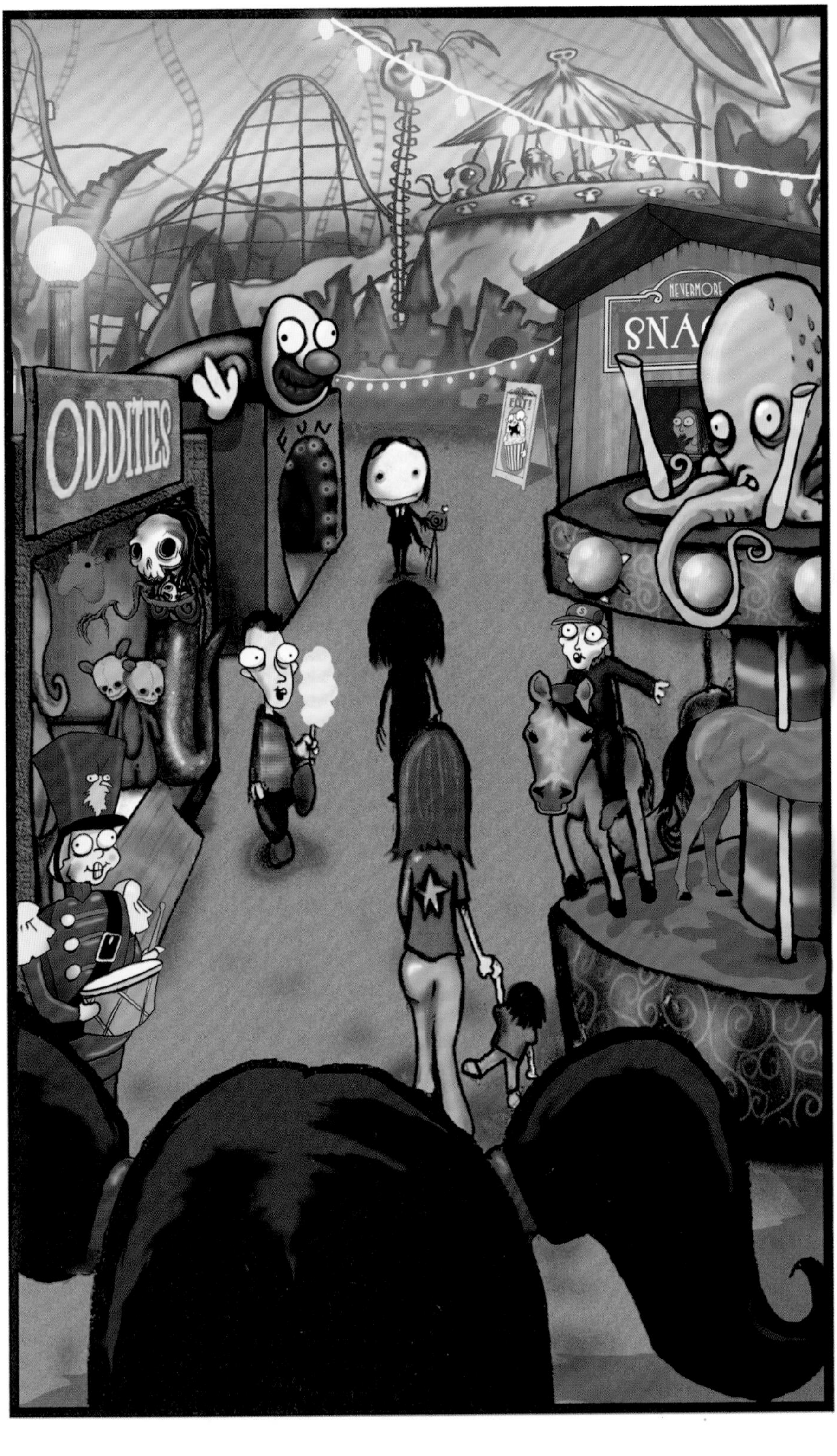
ODDITIES
FUN
NEVERMORE

"Hello dear brother!"
Ragamuffin spoke out.
"I knew this day would come.
Let us fight our final bout."
"No No," responded the Sideways Man.
"This is not how I want it to end.
I feel only love for you my sibling.
Please just be my friend."

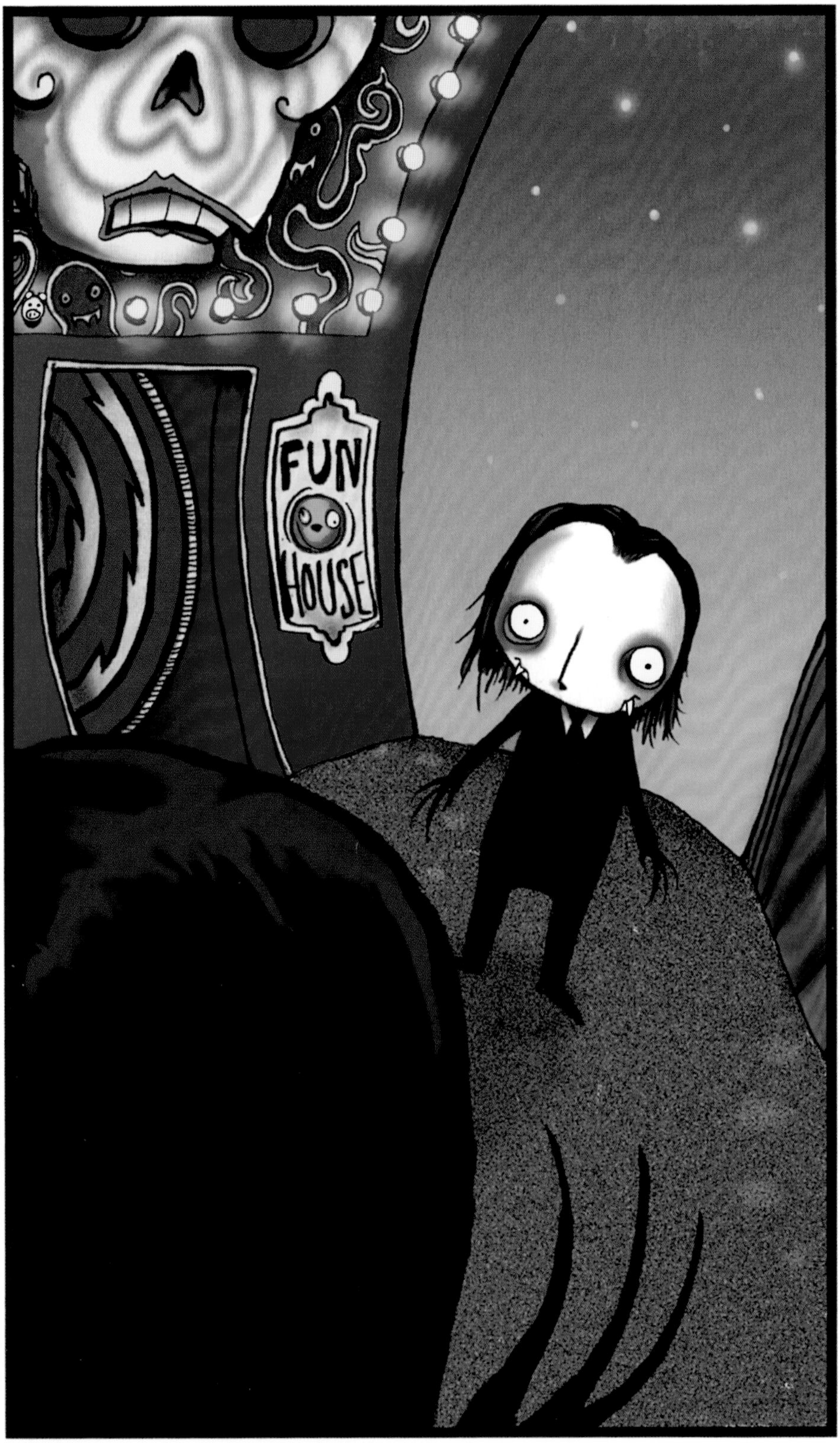
FUN
HOUSE

"You bragged that you're
the greatest killer.
You know that it's not true.
Your lie has been heard
by many.
Now there is only
one thing we can do."
With those last words,
the brothers clashed
into an epic fight.
They both fought bravely,
but only Ragamuffin walked away.
The Sideways Man lost the fight.

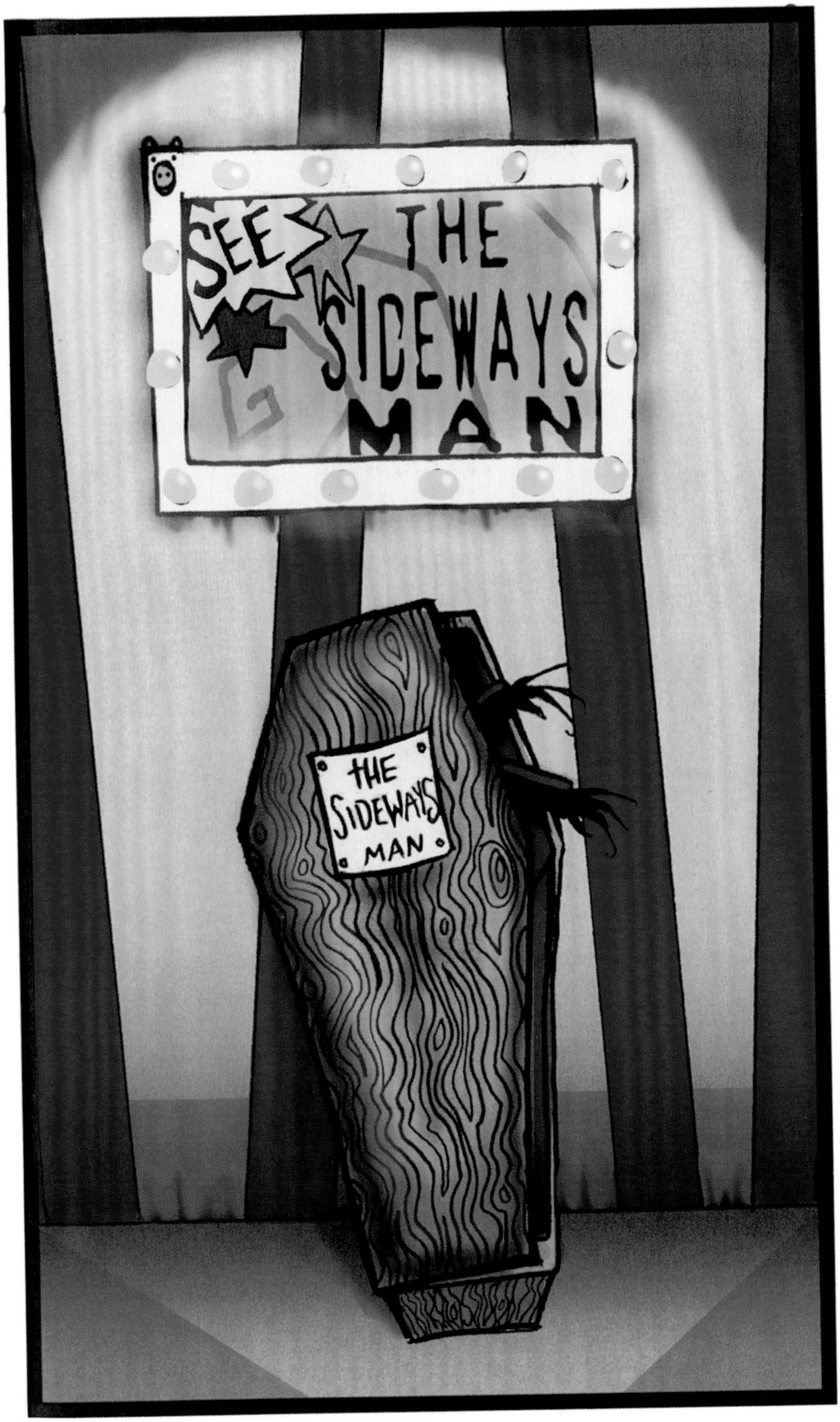
SEE THE SIDEWAYS MAN
THE SIDEWAYS MAN

SOMETHING AT THE WINDOW IS SCRATCHING

A cold December night
as the snow comes down,
sleeping am I –
snug, quiet, not a sound.

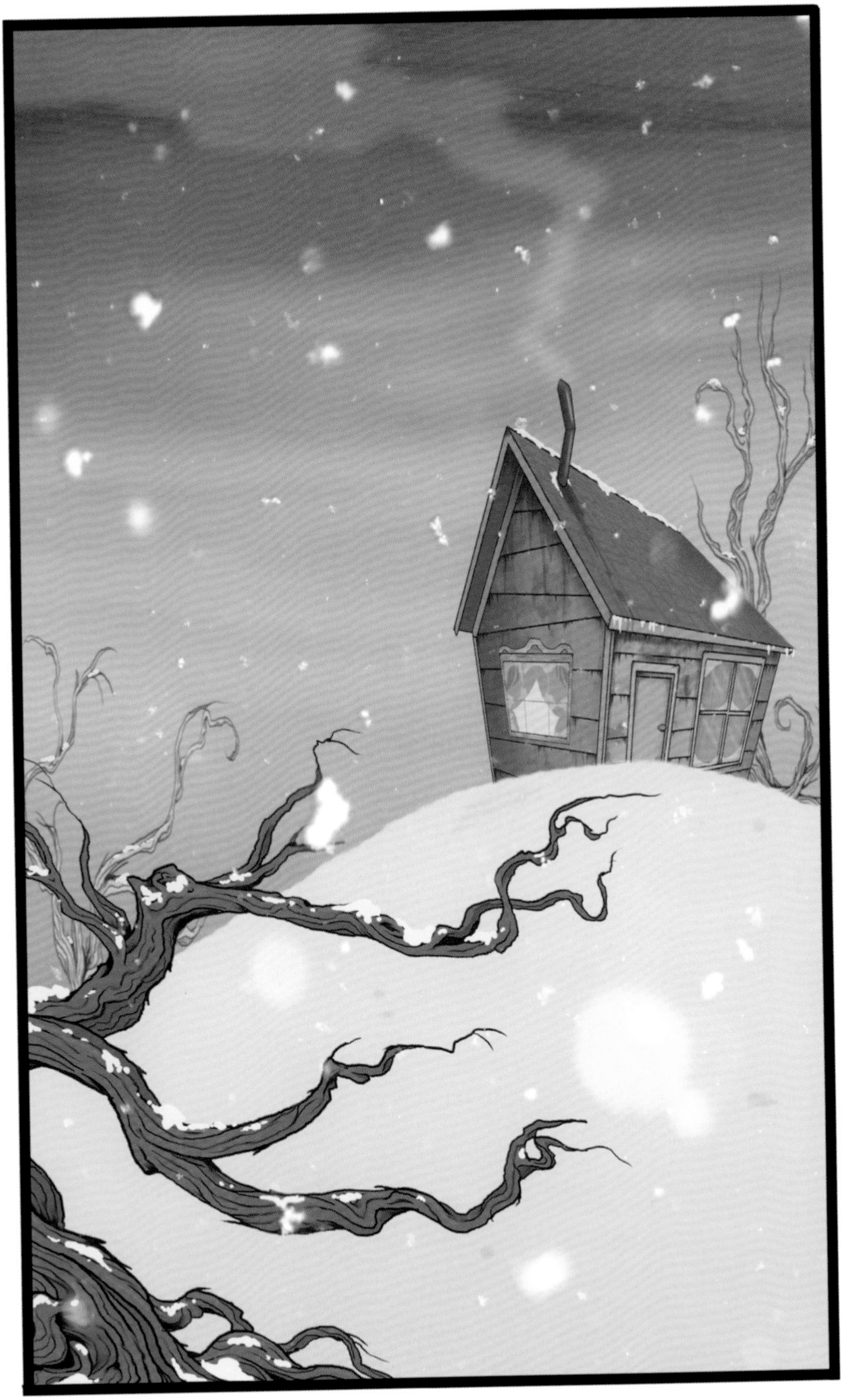

I had long been visited
by Mr. Sandman –
away he took me
to Sleepytime Land.

I dream of
Ghosts, Goblins, and other creepy things,
feeling this fear
a dream like this brings.

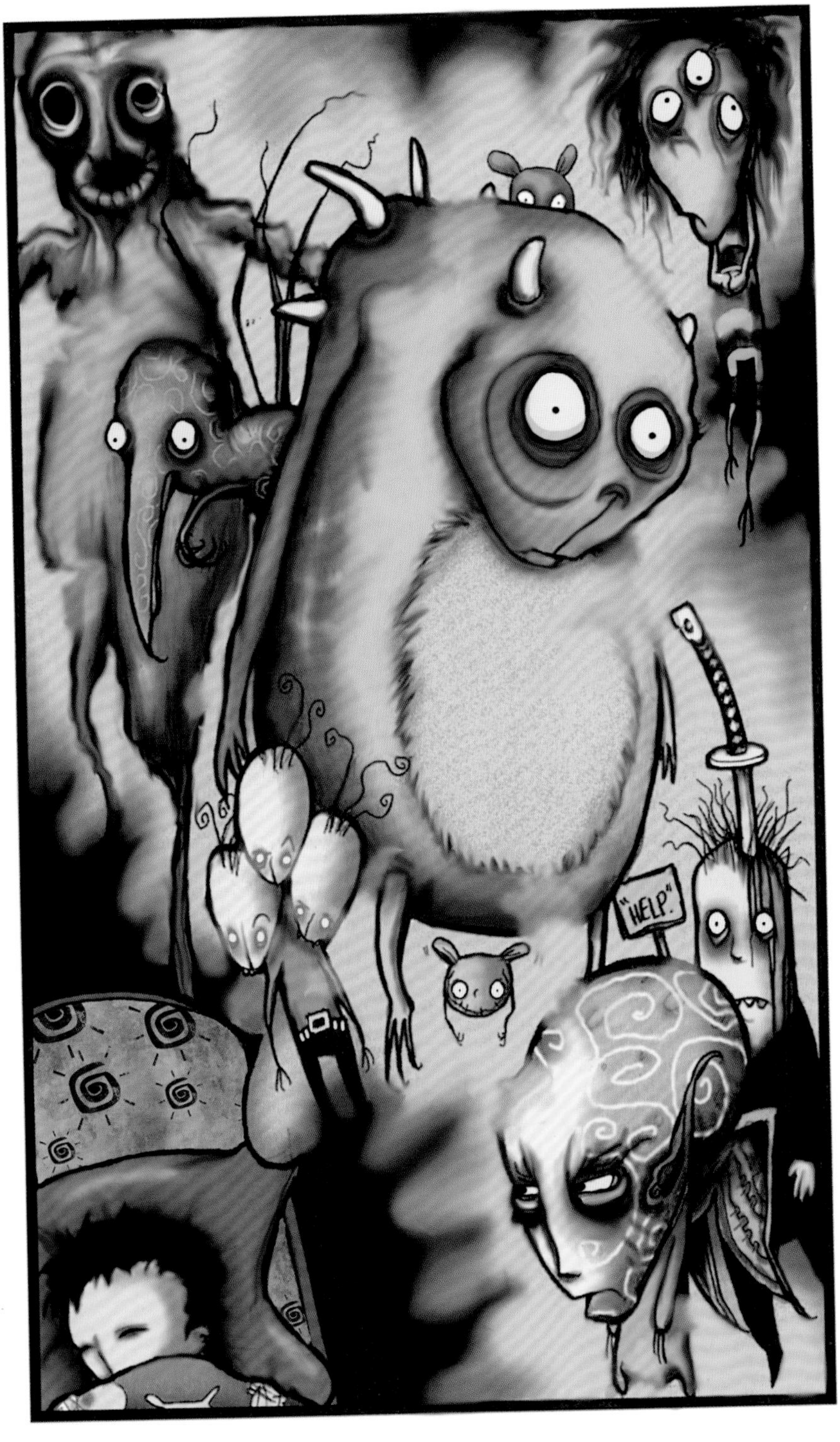
"HELP."

And then suddenly,
as the egg of fear in me
is hatching,
I realize
that something at the window is scratching.

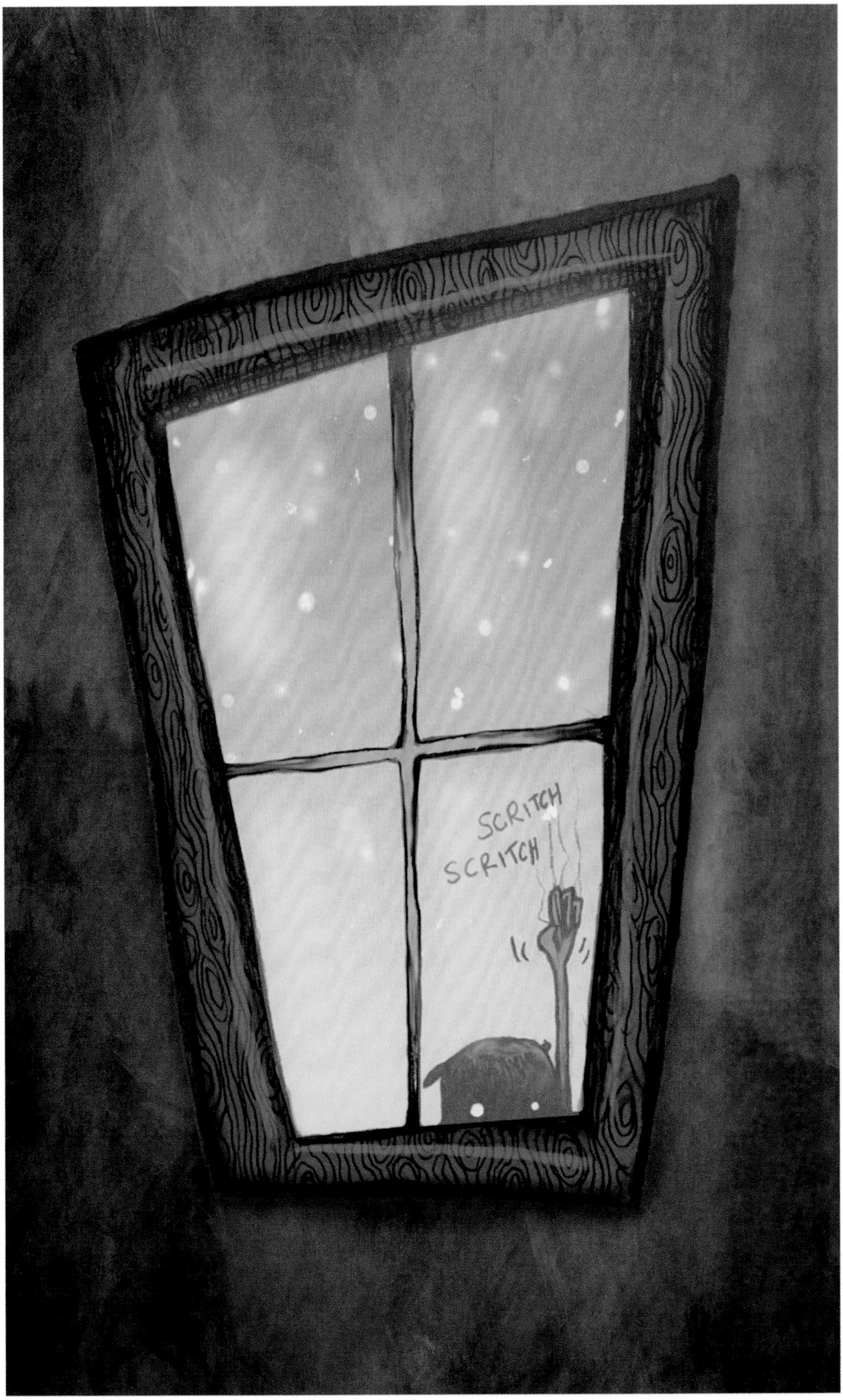
SCRITCH
SCRITCH

Straight up sat I
with my eyes intent.
Watching the window
and what it will vent.
A dark pane of glass
is all that I see,
but I know that I heard it.
What could it be?

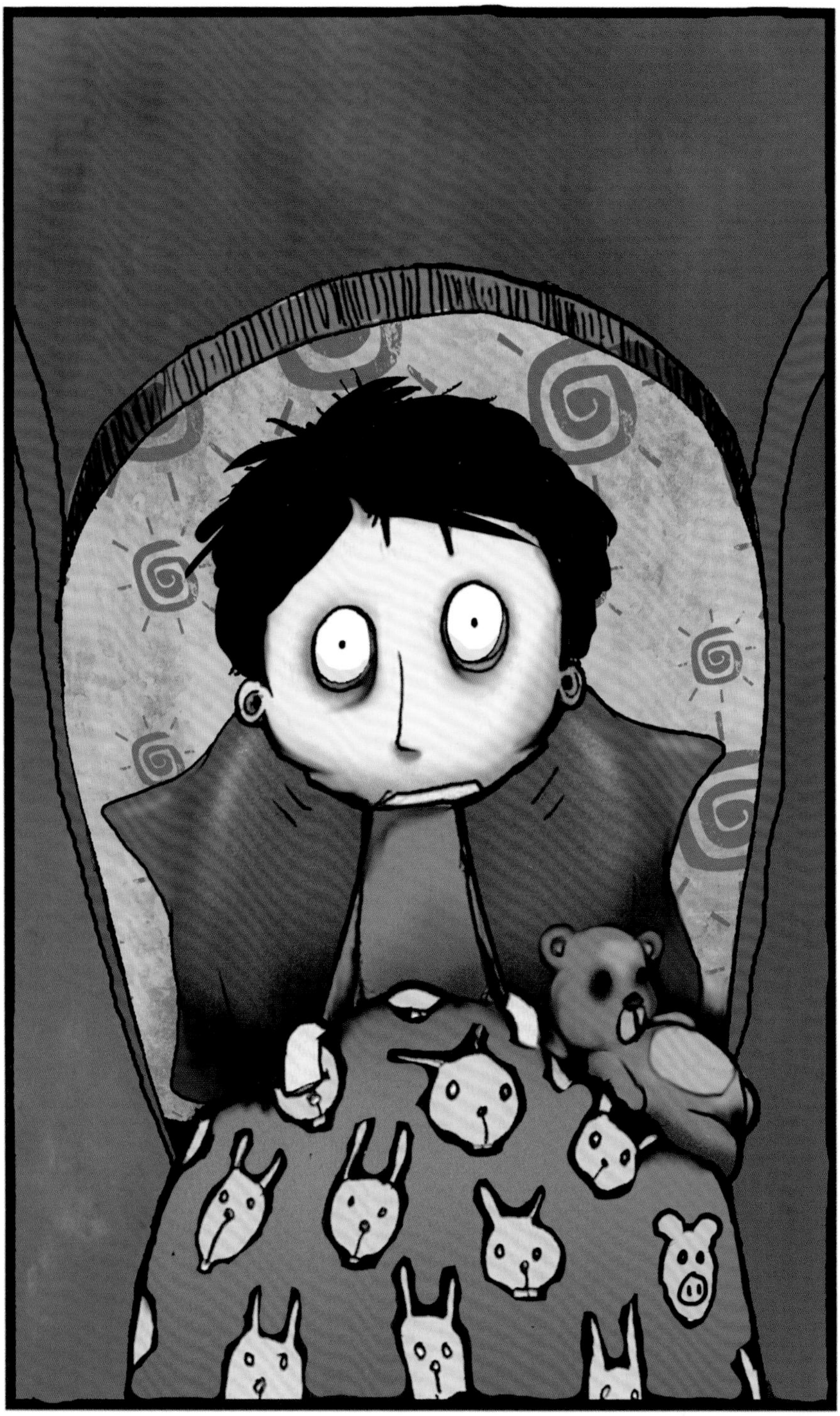

I ventured over to the window
and what should I see?
But an odd little creature
looking back at me.
Sanity left me
and my fear quickly followed suit,
as I felt that this being
was indeed harmless and cute.

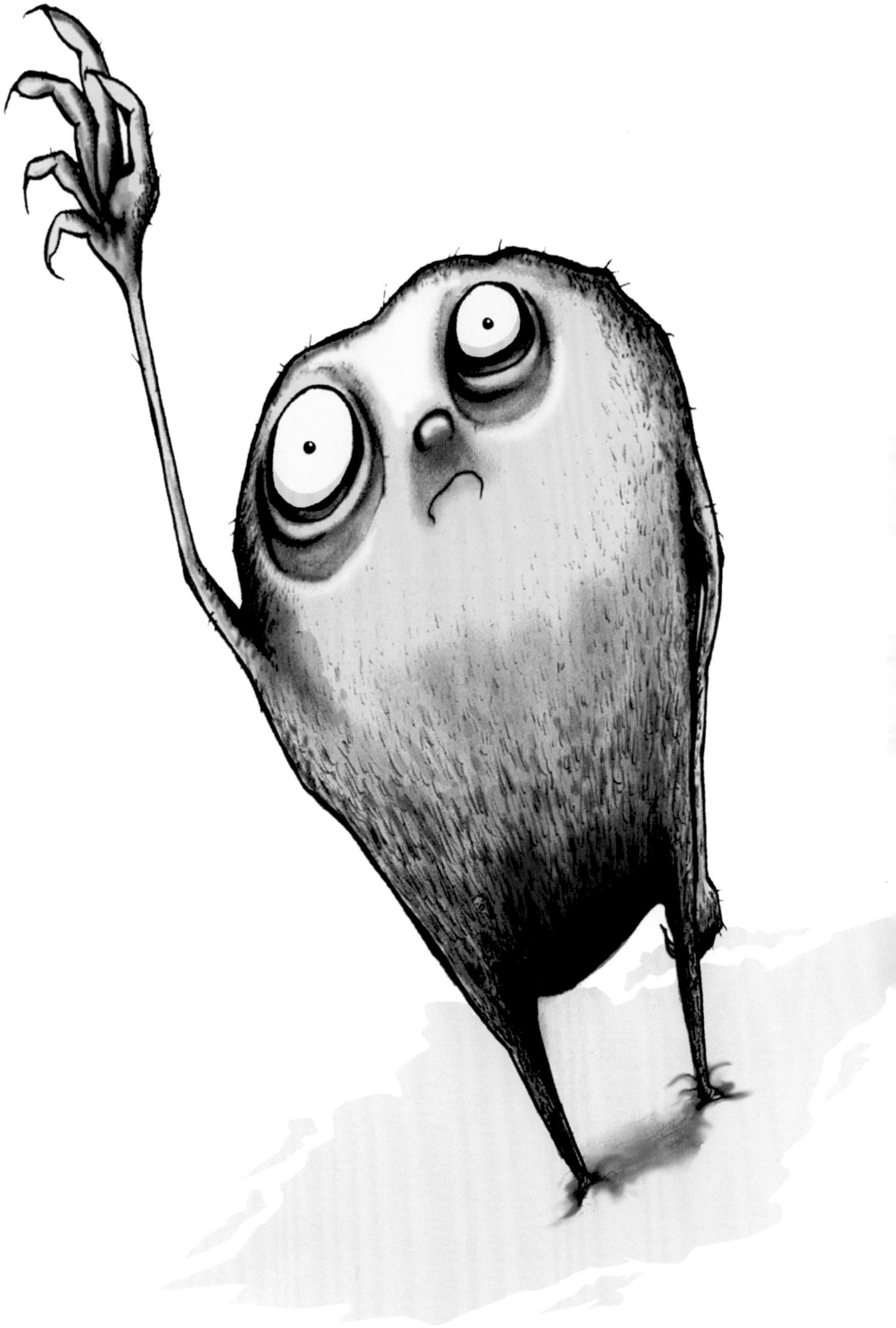

Then the thing spoke
in an eerie little voice.
He was sorry to wake me,
but he hadn't a choice.
"I'm sorry," said he, "to give you such a fright,
but I'm looking for my daddy.
He did not come home this nite."
"You were the last one on his list," the creature
did weep.
"I know that he's been here,
since I found you asleep."

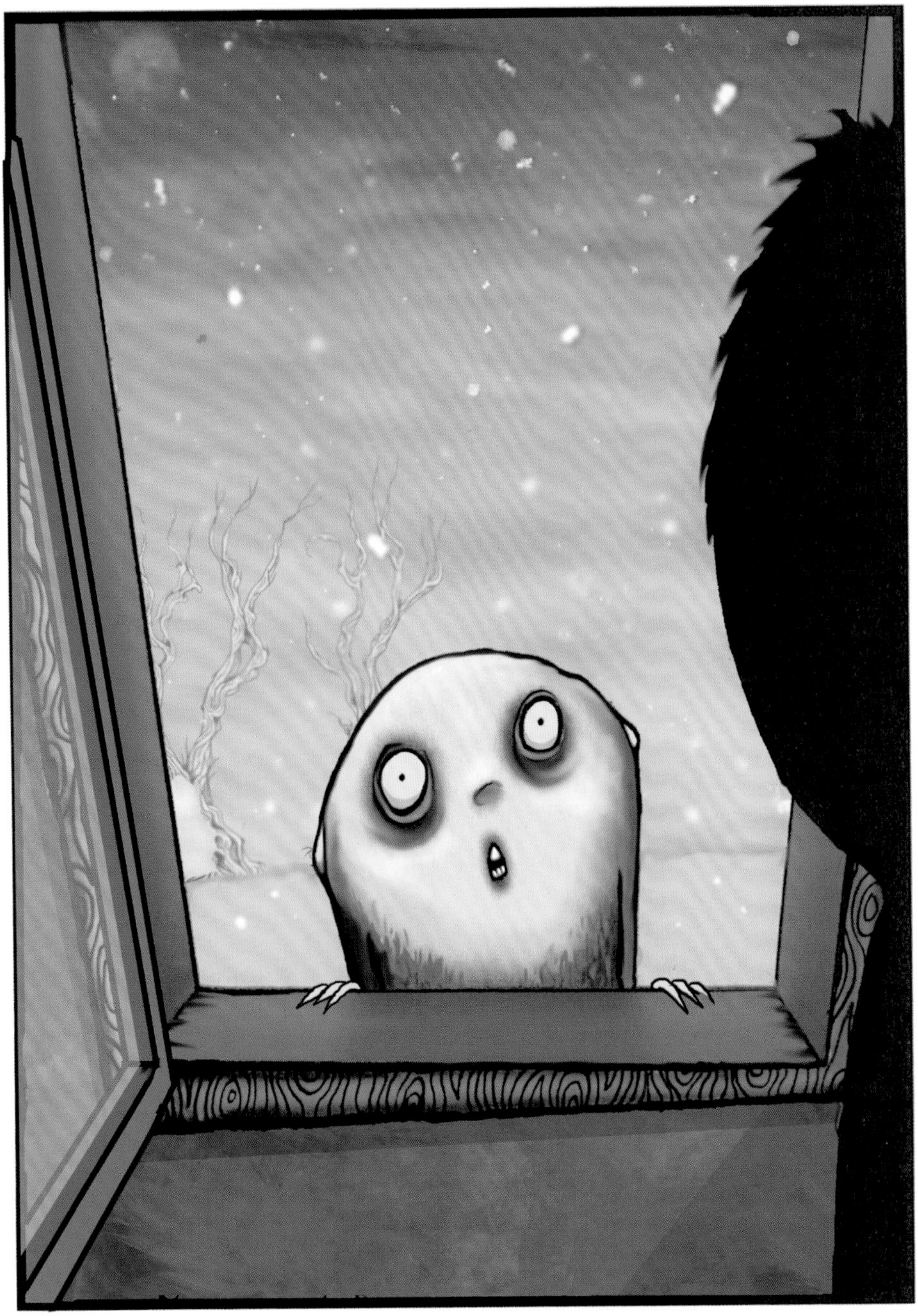

I did not understand
the logic in what he had said.
My visitor knew his dad had been here
cause he found me in bed.
Just then I noticed
some footsteps out in the snow.
I jumped out the window
and away we did go.

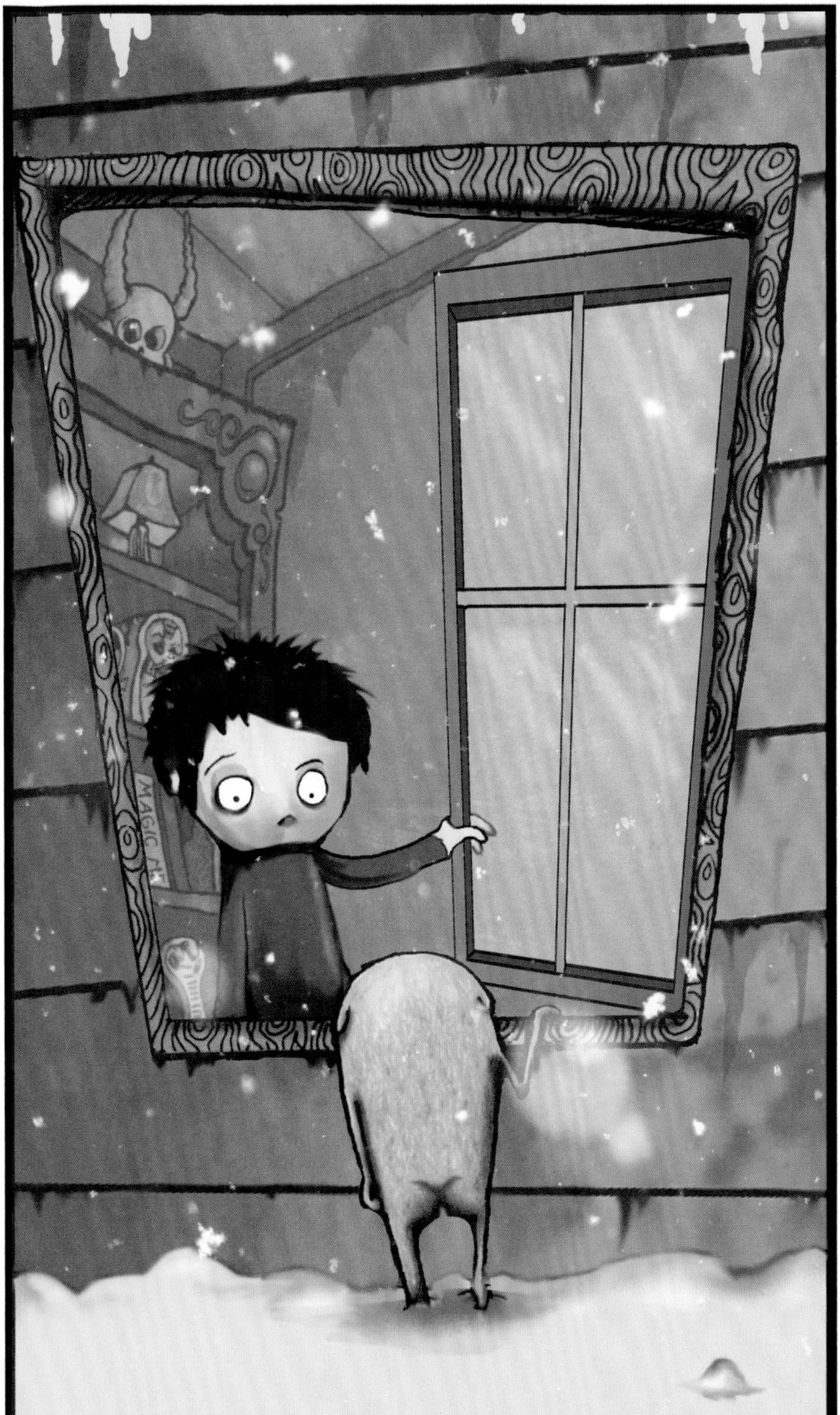
MAGIC

We hadn't walked far
before we found something
very sad.
There in the snow,
was this poor orphan's dad.
It all made sense now
what the little monster had said.
The Sandman was his daddy
and now he was dead.
After he had left me from making me nap,
he froze to death,
caught in an old bear trap.

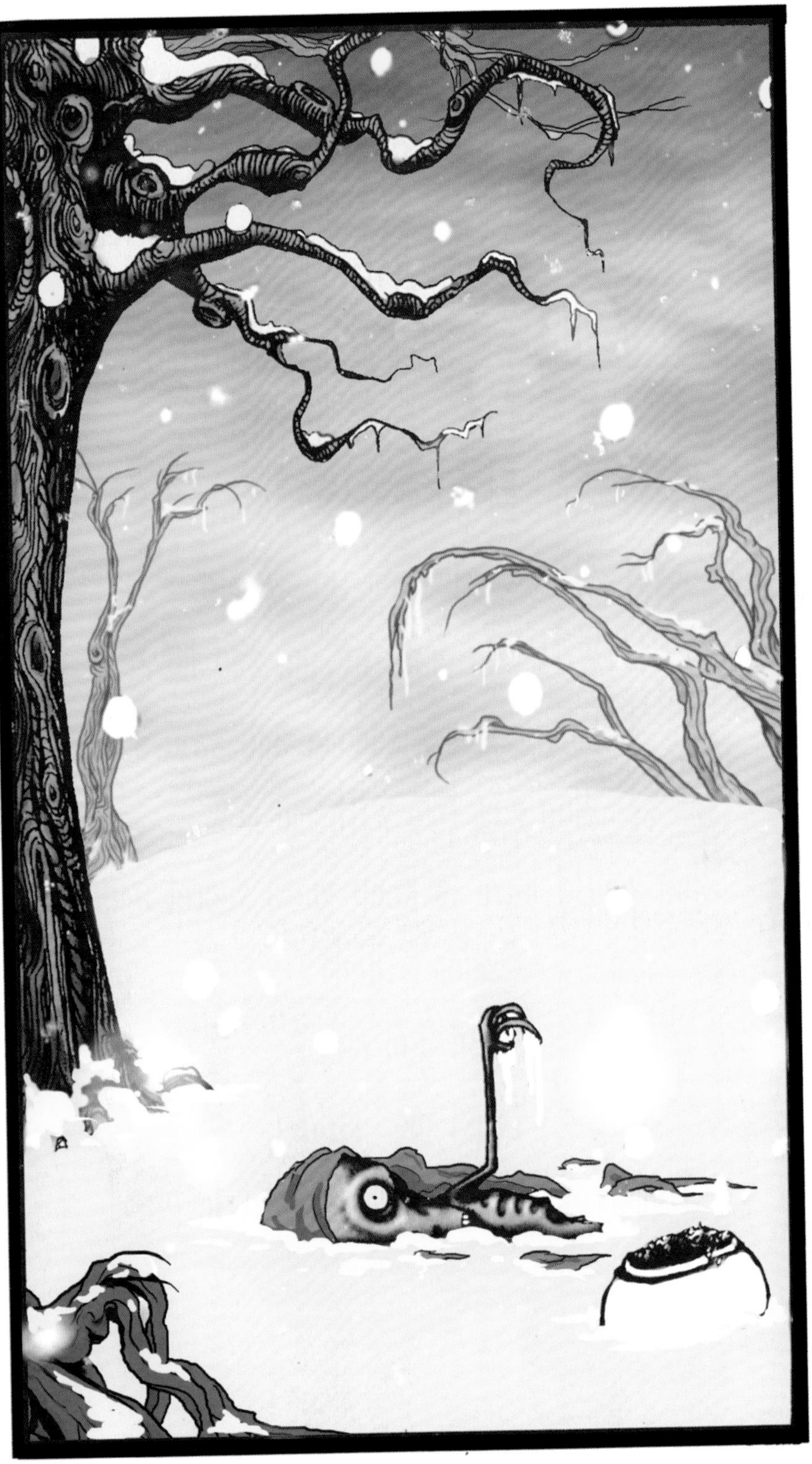

"No! No! No!"
the little Sandman began crying.
I told him it would be ok,
but he knew I was lying.
"I'm so alone in this world.
Who will take care of me and how?"
I thought for a second and said,
"You can live with me now."
"You would have to keep me a secret and I
don't think
that you can."
"Trust me," said I.
"Tomorrow you will see my little plan."

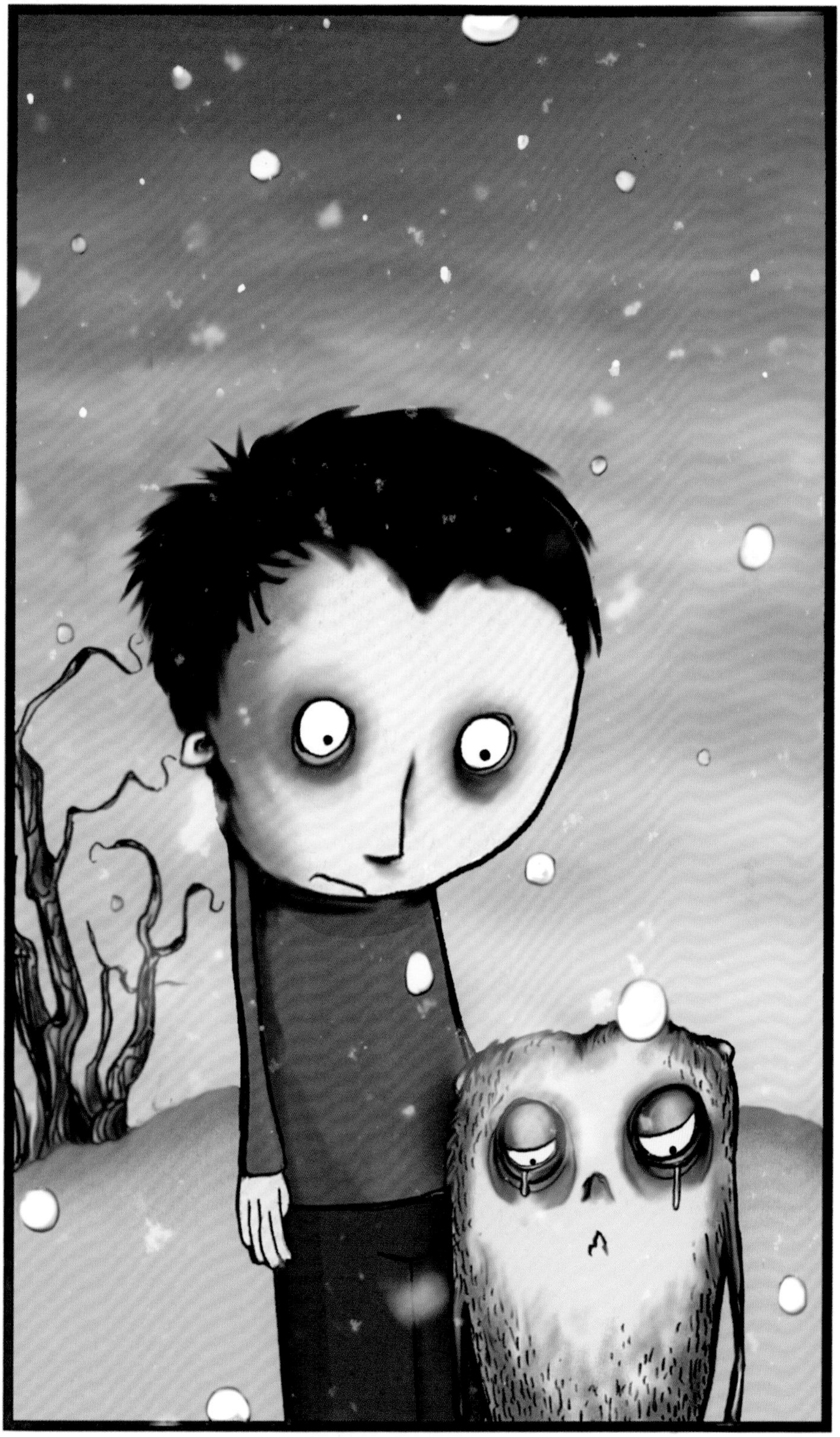

The very next morning
I put my plan into action.
Tricking my parents
would be a very hard faction.
As around the breakfast table
we all sat,
I said, "Mom and Dad....
Meet our new cat."

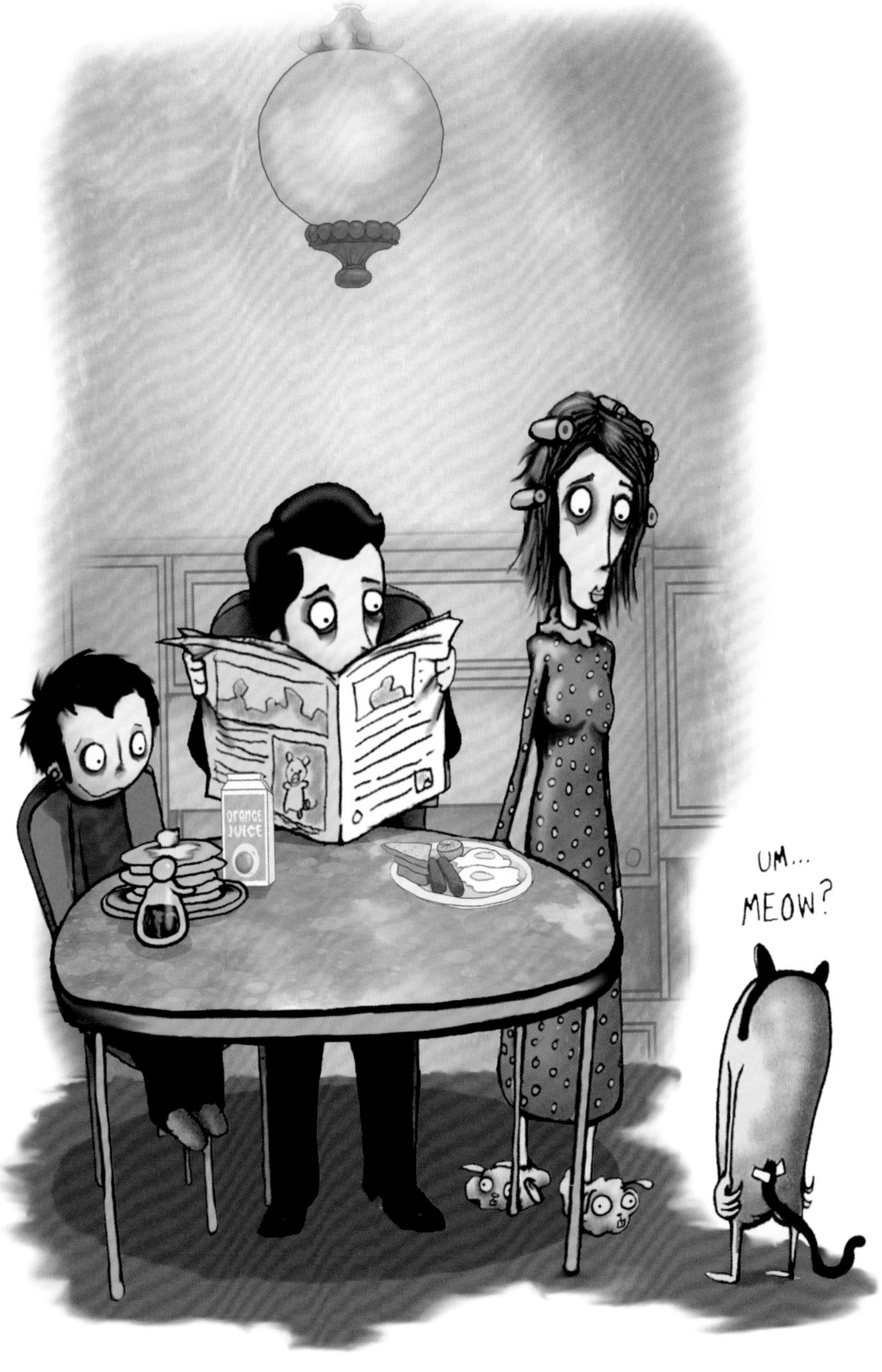

ORANGE JUICE
UM...
MEOW?

MR SEEPHIS

Poor Mr. Seephis
king of the bear people,
wearing a self-proclaimed crown
atop a homemade steeple.
All you want are bears to care about you –
warm, furry and kind.
Except for BoBo the killer bear
who was not so inclined.

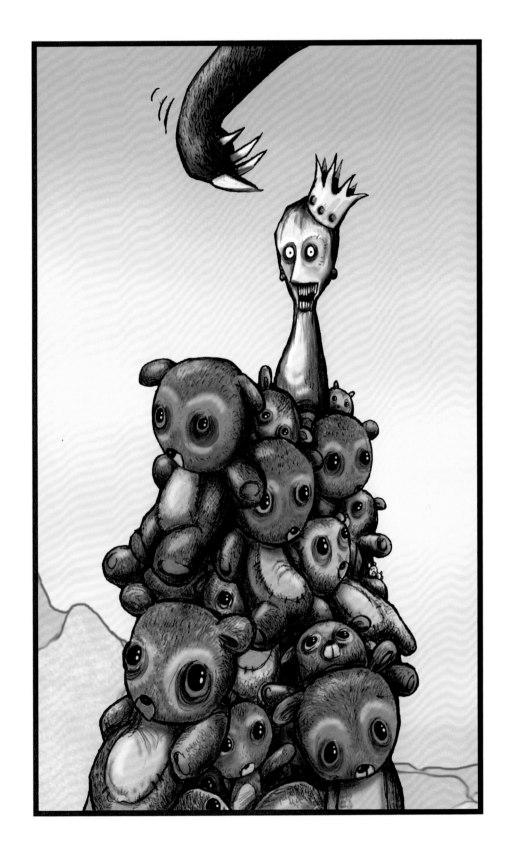

LITTLE LISA LOVERBUMPS

Little Lisa Loverbumps
was the closest girl to me.
Until one day without warning
she walked out into the sea.

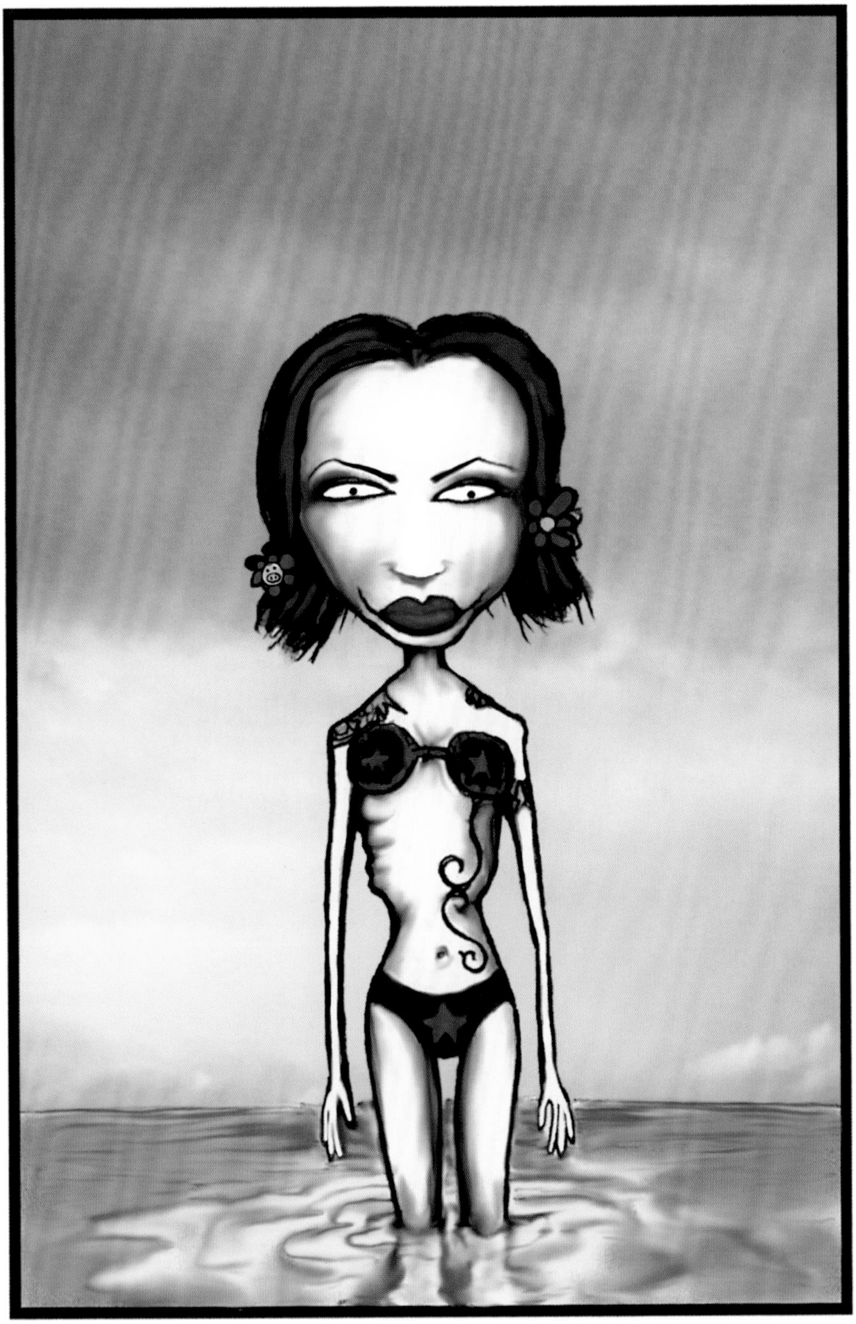

At first I thought she was joking –
funniest thing I'd seen all day –
but the joke was over quickly
as I watched her float away.

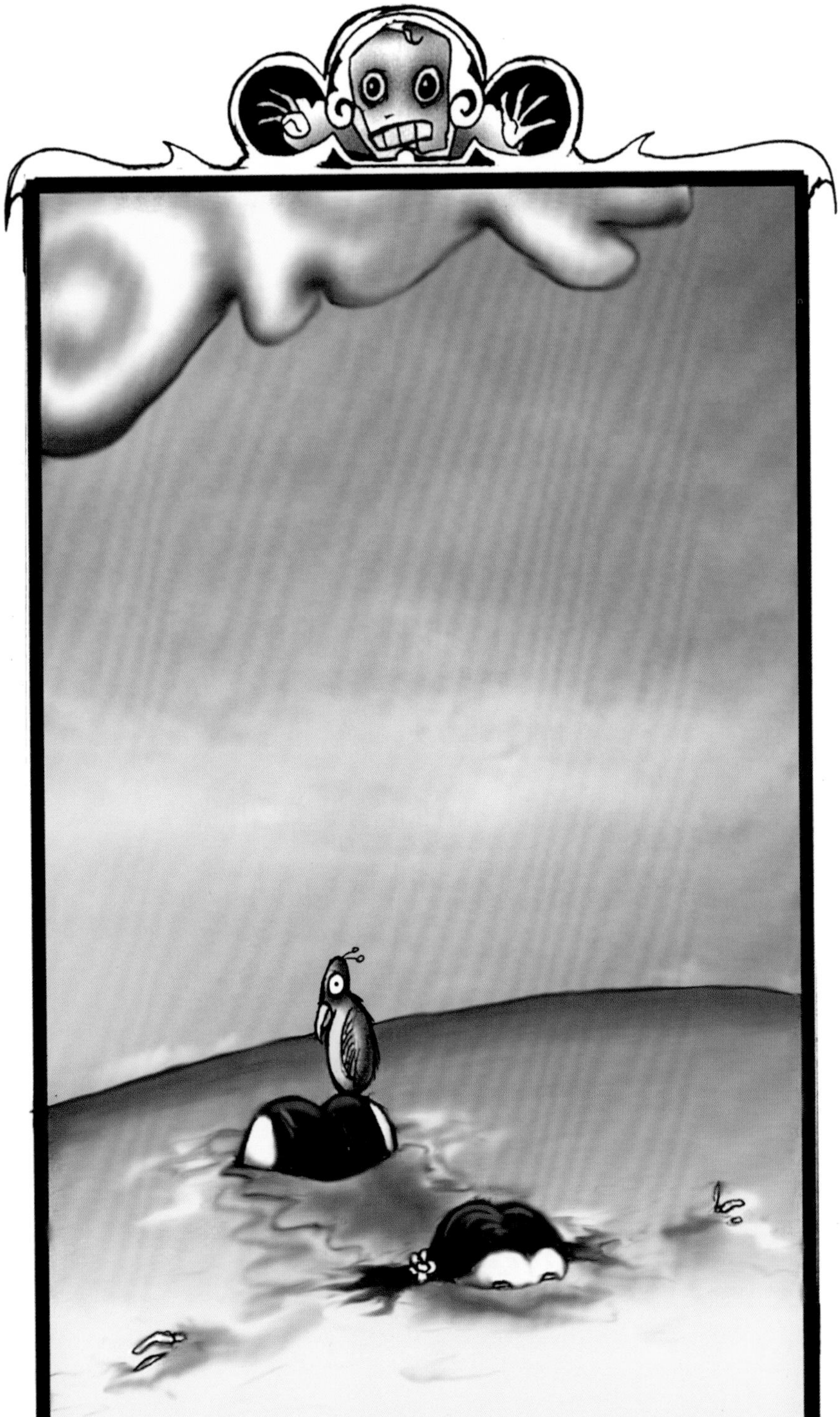

PETER THE PIRATE SQUID

There's not a whole lot he did –
Peter, the pirate squid.

THE GHOST IN THE SPIDER

There was once a spider
with a ghost inside her –
and what a happy ghost it was.
When asked why the ghost did it,
he had to admit it.
All he would say was "because."

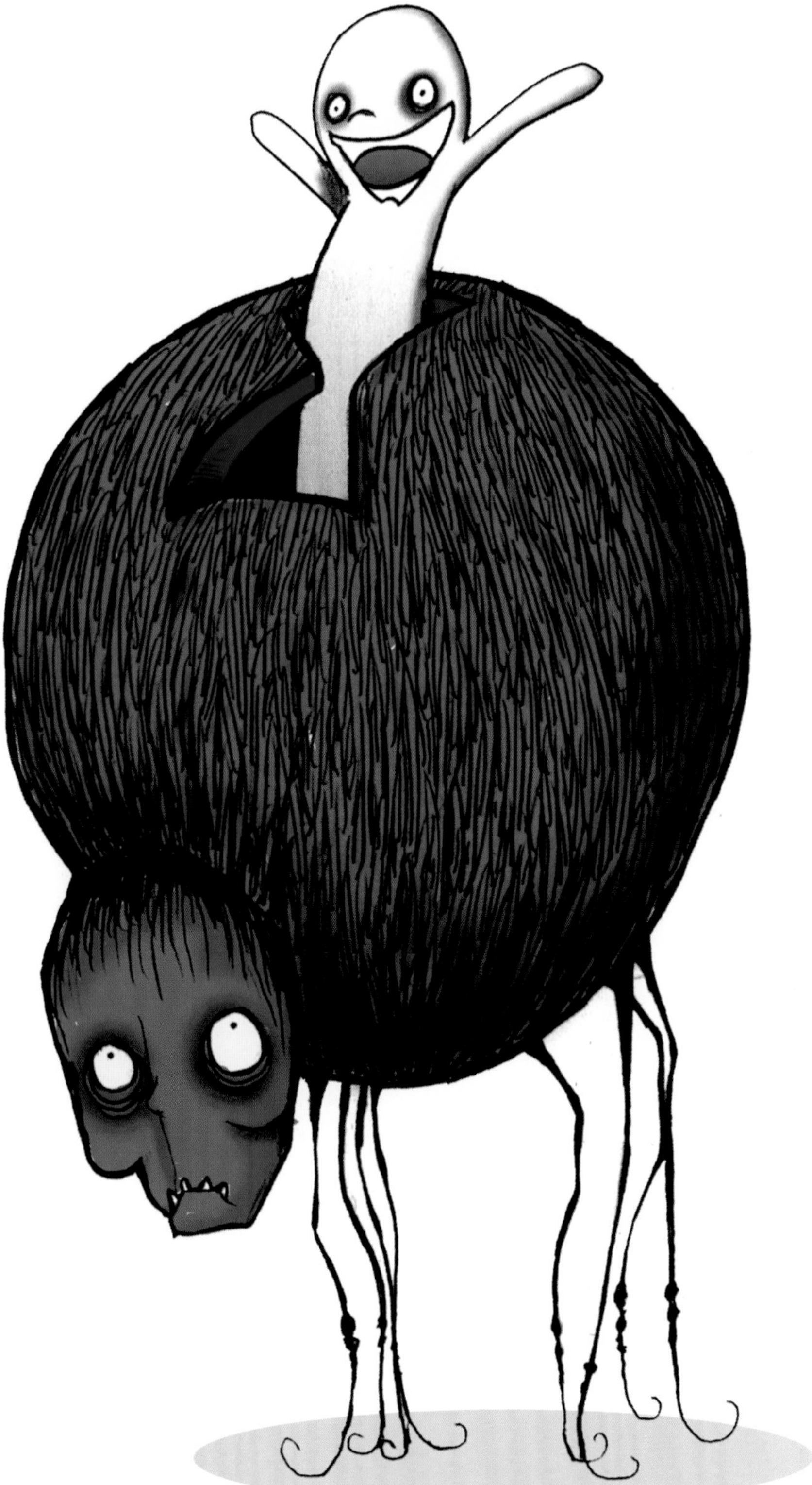

So on the spider went
with a wondering intent
as to why the ghost chose her.
Over the flowers
the spider walked for hours
with the ghost as a passenger.

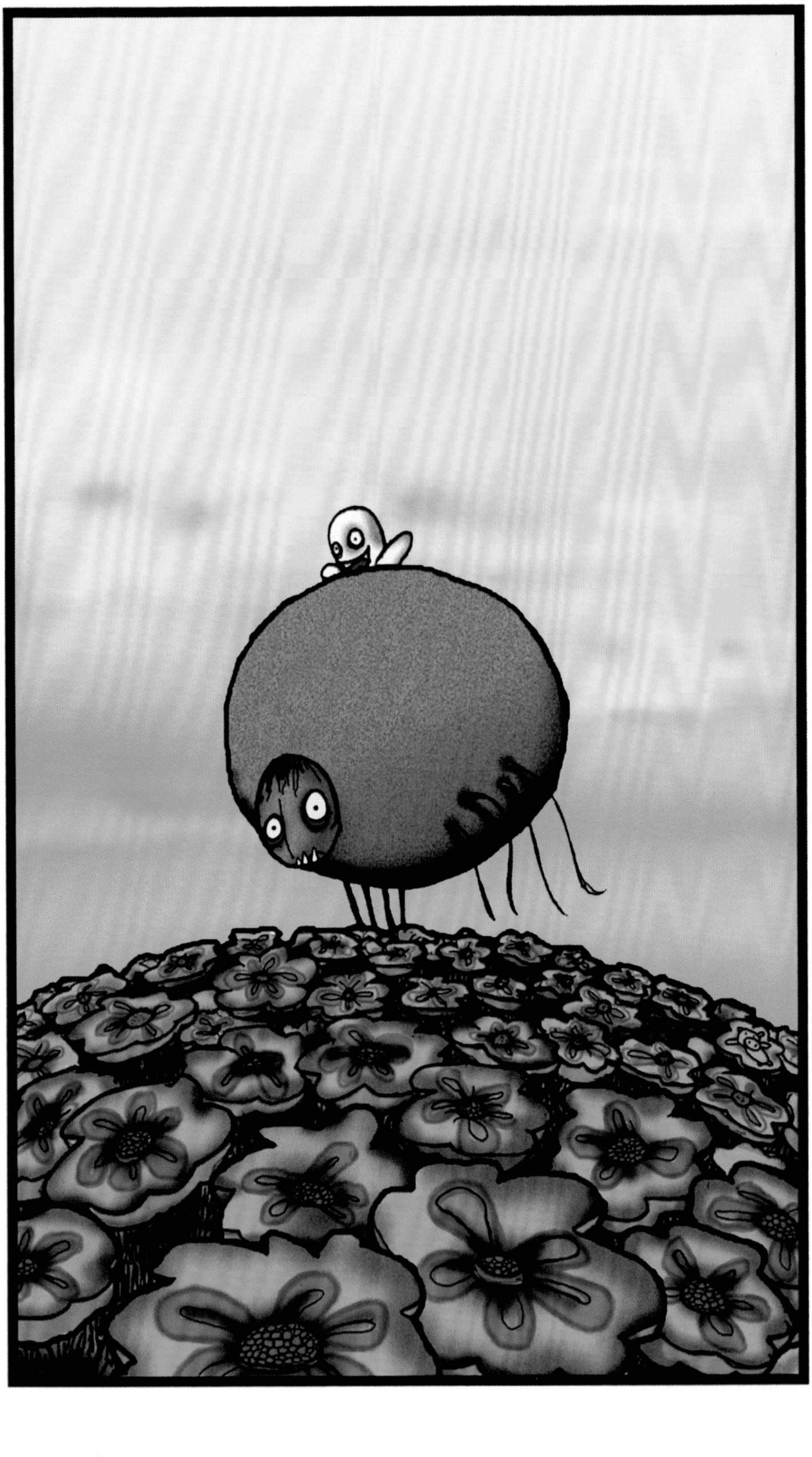

So then the spider
and its spectral rider
came across the spiders three.
The arachnids made fun
of their brethren one
so off again they would be.

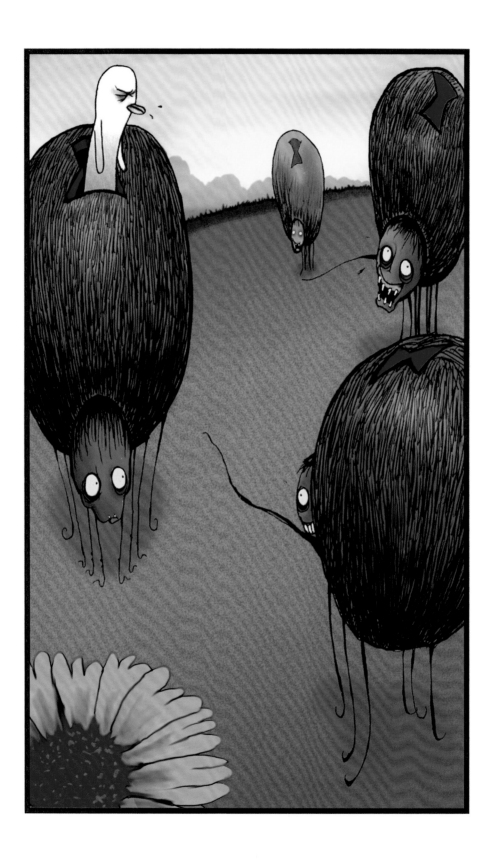

They never quit
kept on walking it –
into the distance they went.
Never finding acceptance –
they haven't been seen since,
as forced away they were sent.

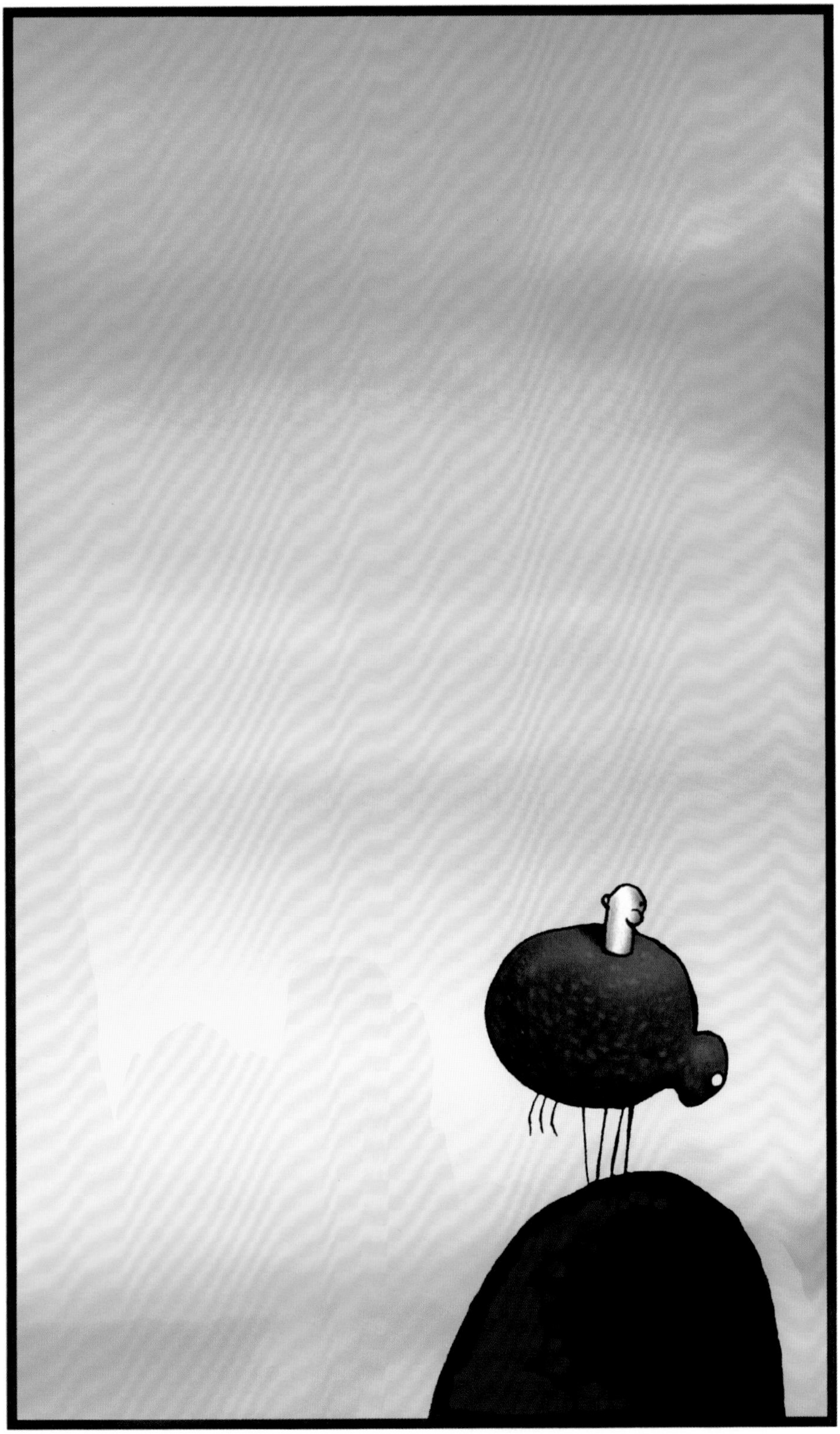

PEAR HEAD MAN AND BREAD BOY

Nature did not have a plan
when it created
the Pear Head Man.
He had one friend
who was made of bread,
but the birdies ate him.
Now he's dead.

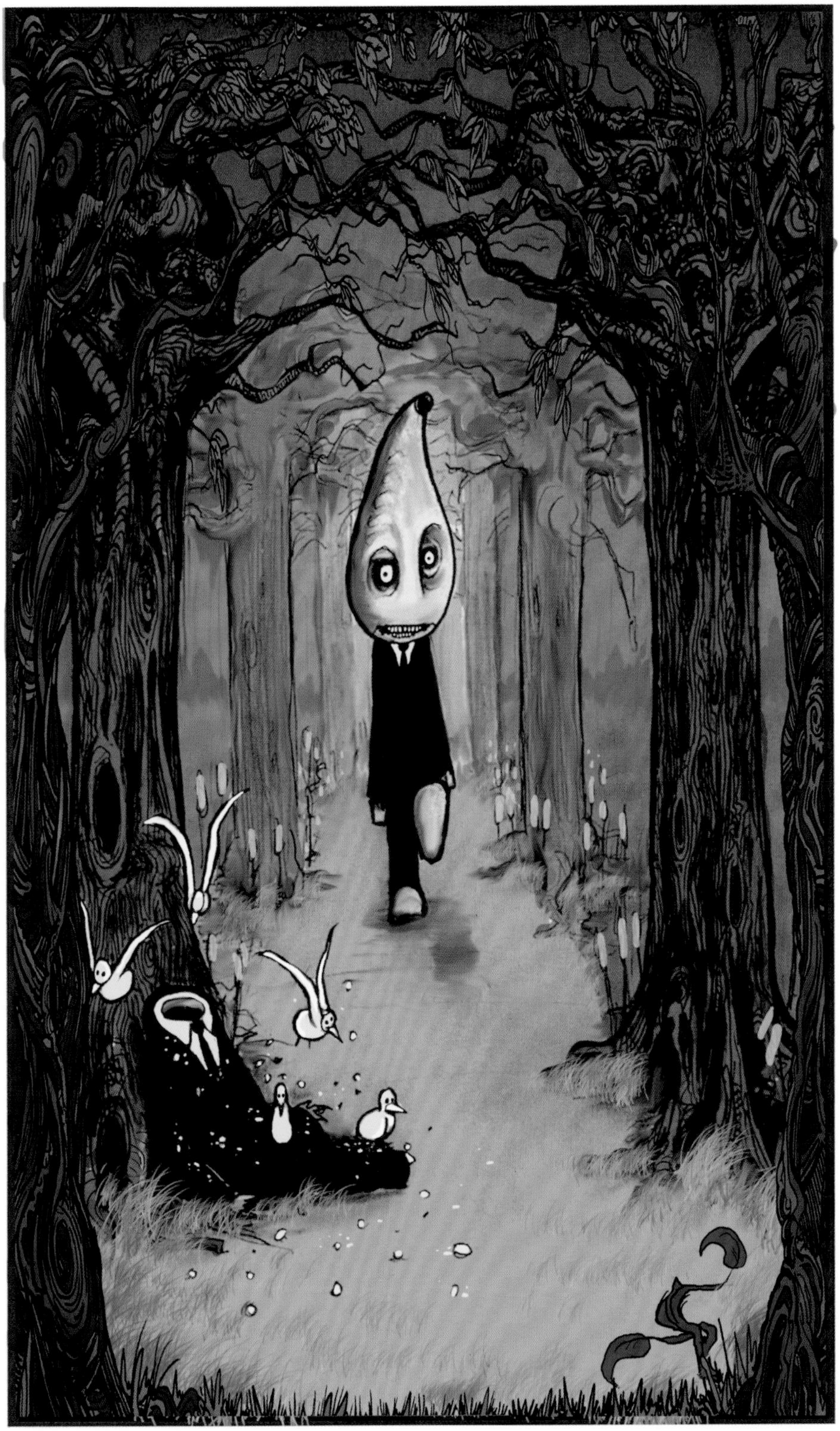

THE ALIEN BALLERINA

No one believes me
that I had seen a
happy dancing
alien ballerina.
It danced very badly
as though it were stiff.
It stopped dancing completely
after it went off the cliff.

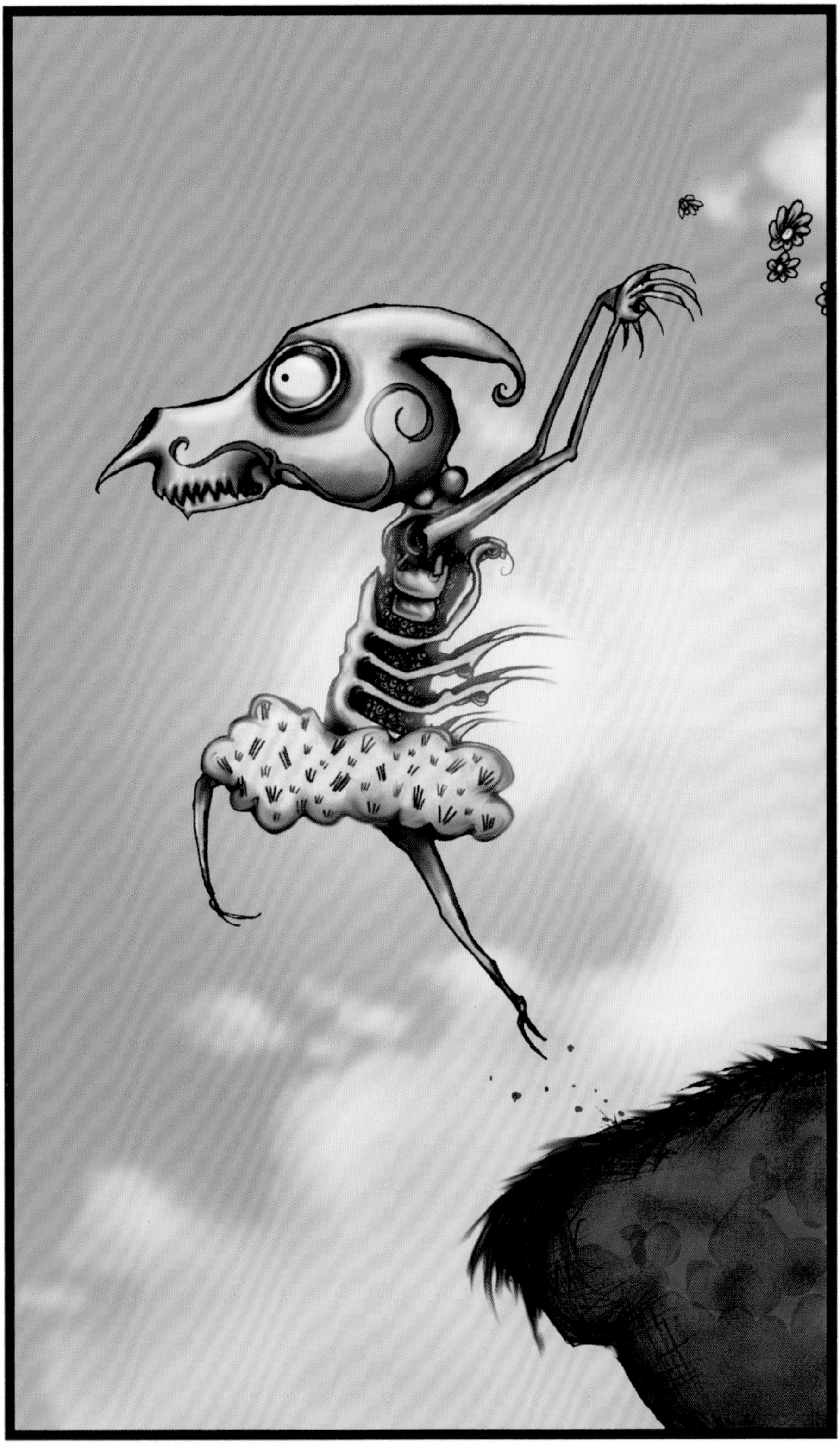

THE BUNNY CAME BACK

Billy had a bunny
that he loved very much.
He'd hug him, pet him
and squeeze him and such.

One day Billy awoke
to an awfully strange whiff
and ventured to find
that his bunny was stiff.

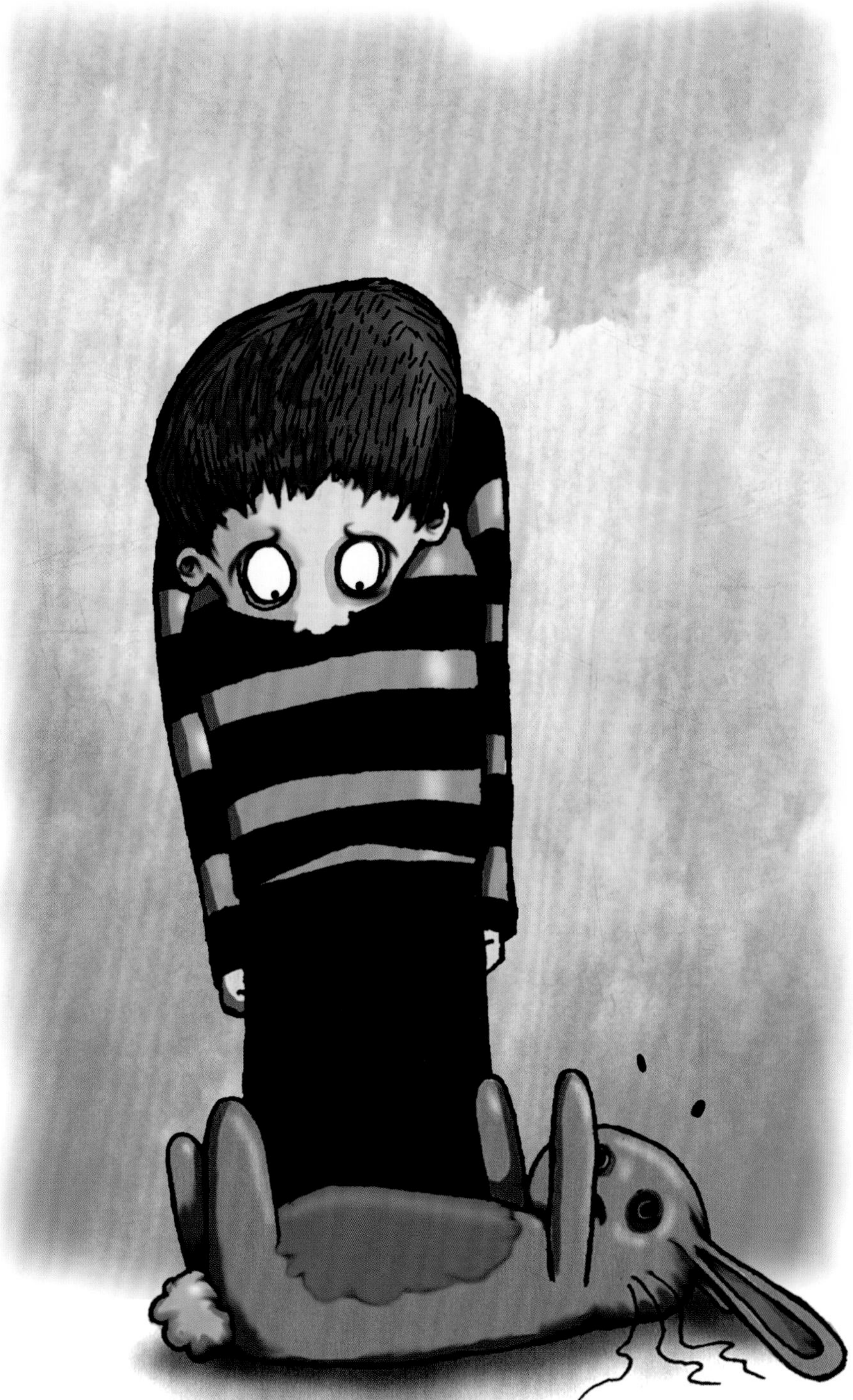

"Mommy! Mommy!" cried Billy.
"My bunny looks weird."
Billy's mother went to find their pet
exactly how she had feared.
In a box the bunny was put
for Billy to carry
and off they hurried
to the Pet Cemetery.

With sadness and tears
the bunny was put into the ground.
Billy just stared quietly
at the buried bunny mound.

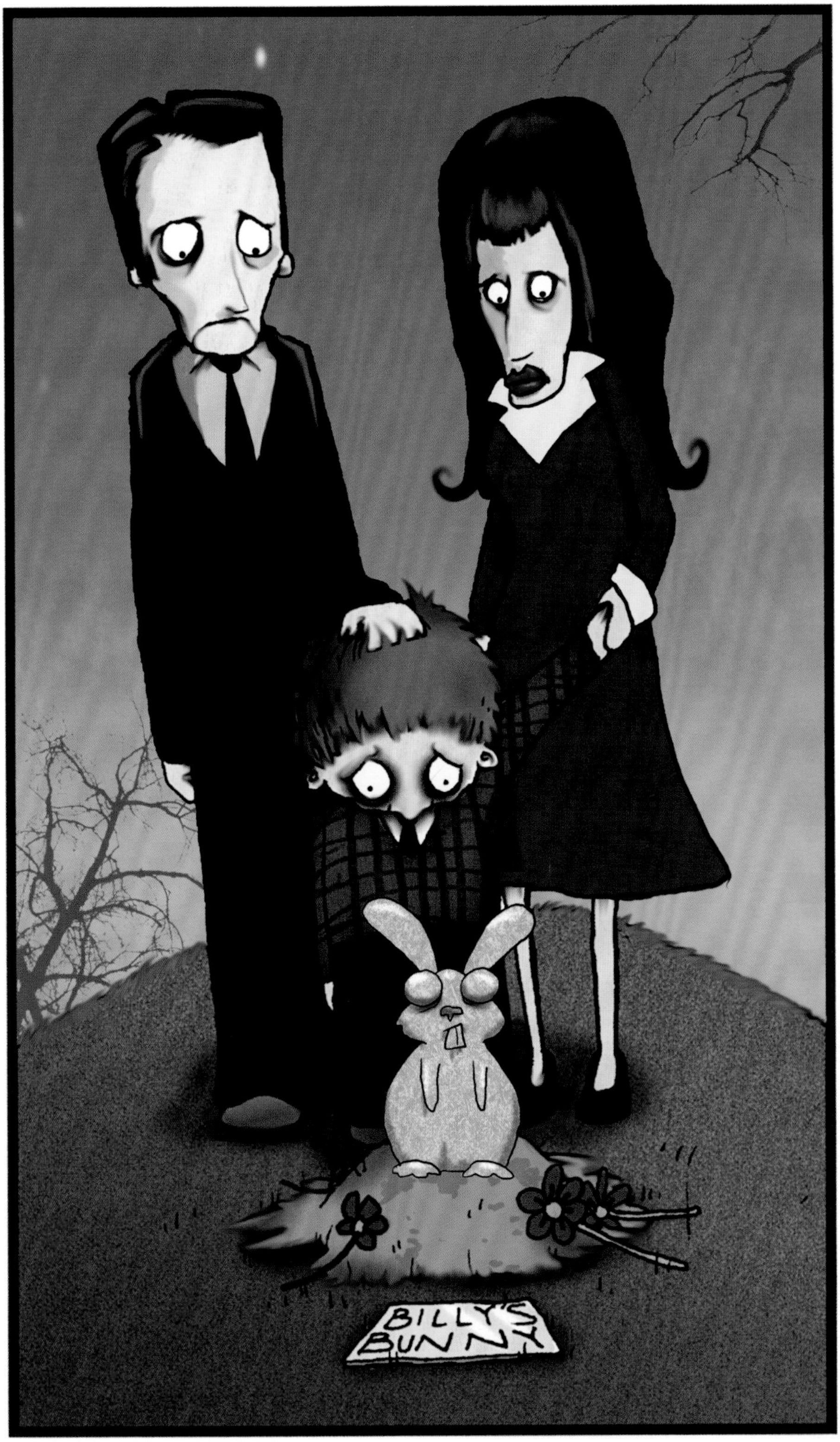
BILLY'S BUNNY

The very next morning
as dawn began to crack,
they opened the door
to find
the bunny came back.
All were speechless
as to what should be said –
how the bunny came back
even though it was dead.

No one could understand
how or why this could be –
but away they went back
and again buried that bunny.
Everyone stood there
just quietly nervous,
hoping and praying
this would be the last service.

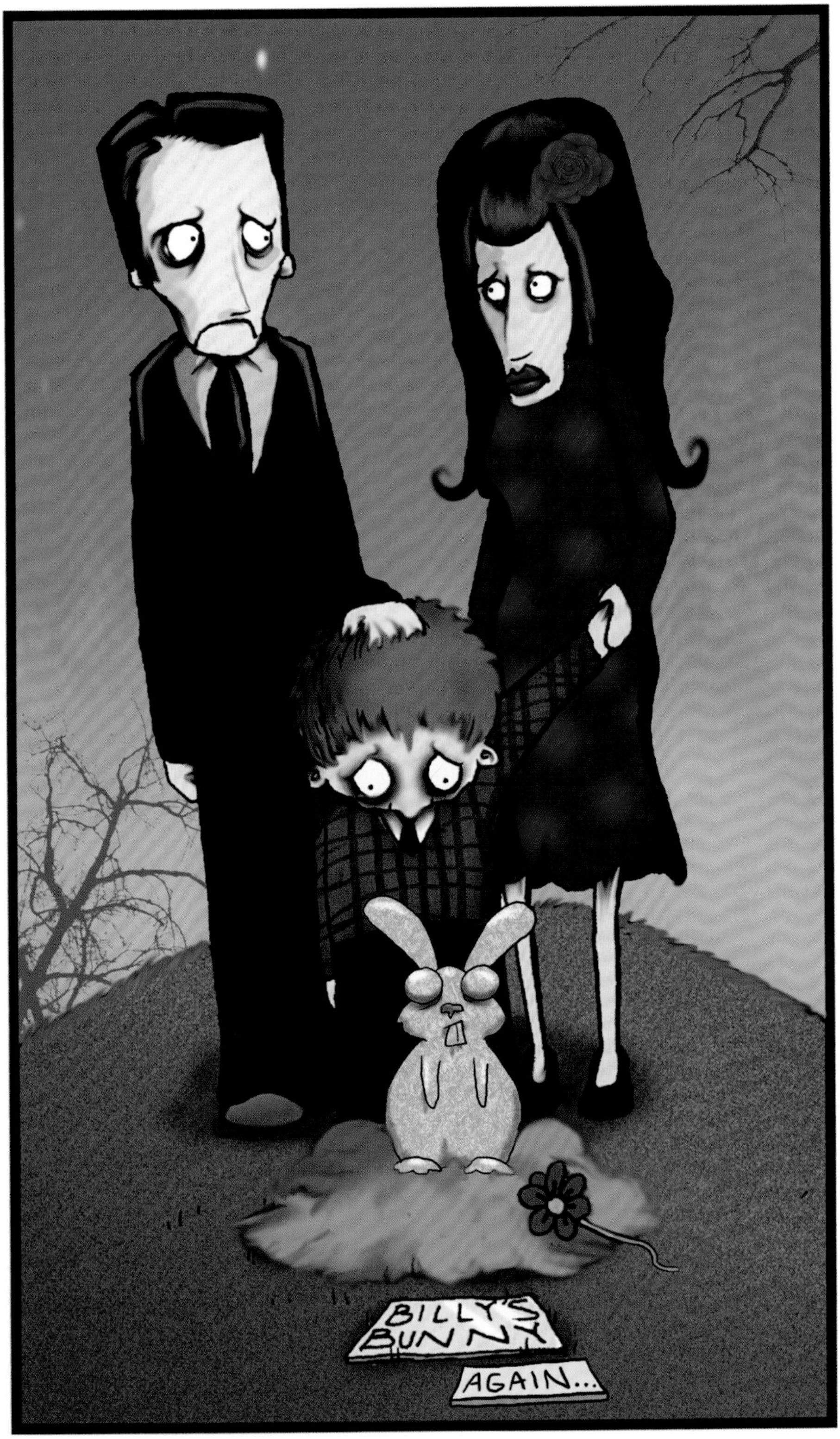
BILLY'S BUNNY
AGAIN...

THE CAPTAIN

A hole in the boat
made it no longer float
so into the sea it sank.
Luckily, a little island was found –
the captain wasn't to be drowned –
but on another problem he could bank.

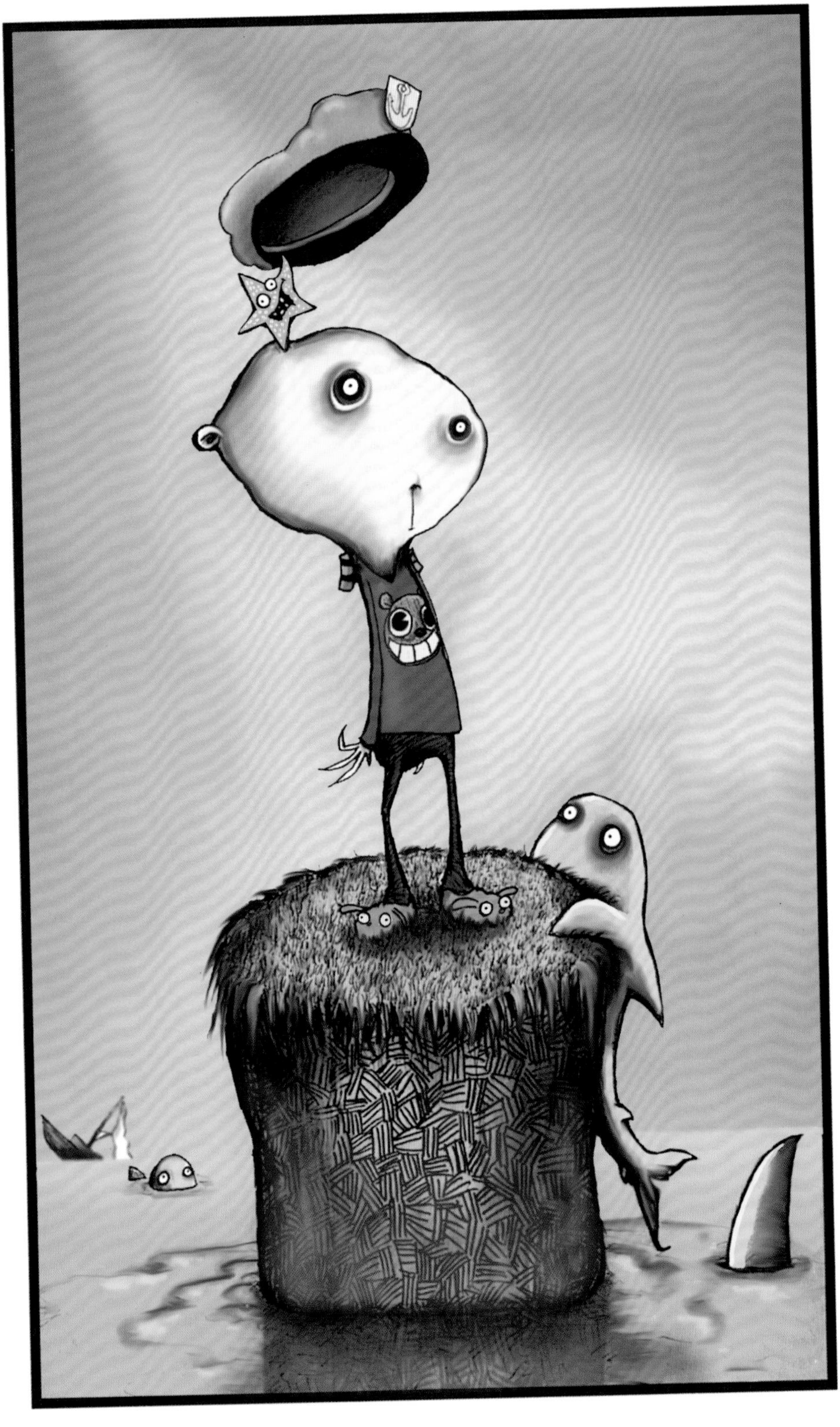

DEVIL BUNNY

A devil holding a bunny...
holding a devil...
holding a bunny...
holding a devil...
holding a bunny...
I'm so sorry
that this is
not funny.

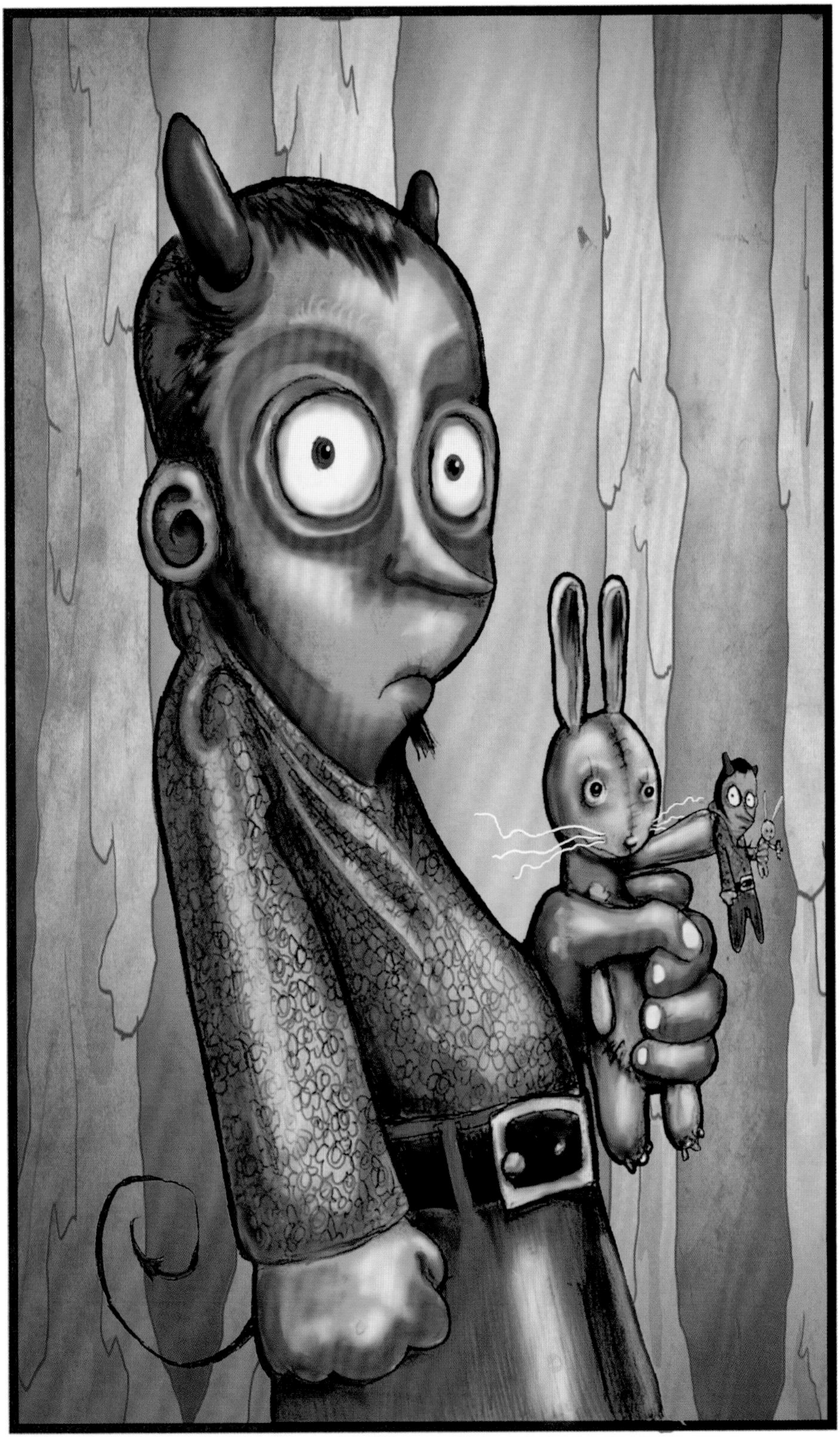

THE REINDEER AND THE BUMBLE BEE

One of the weirdest things
that you could ever see
was a reindeer in love
with a bumble bee.
No one was sure how
or even remembered why –
how a creature that could walk
loved a creature that could fly.

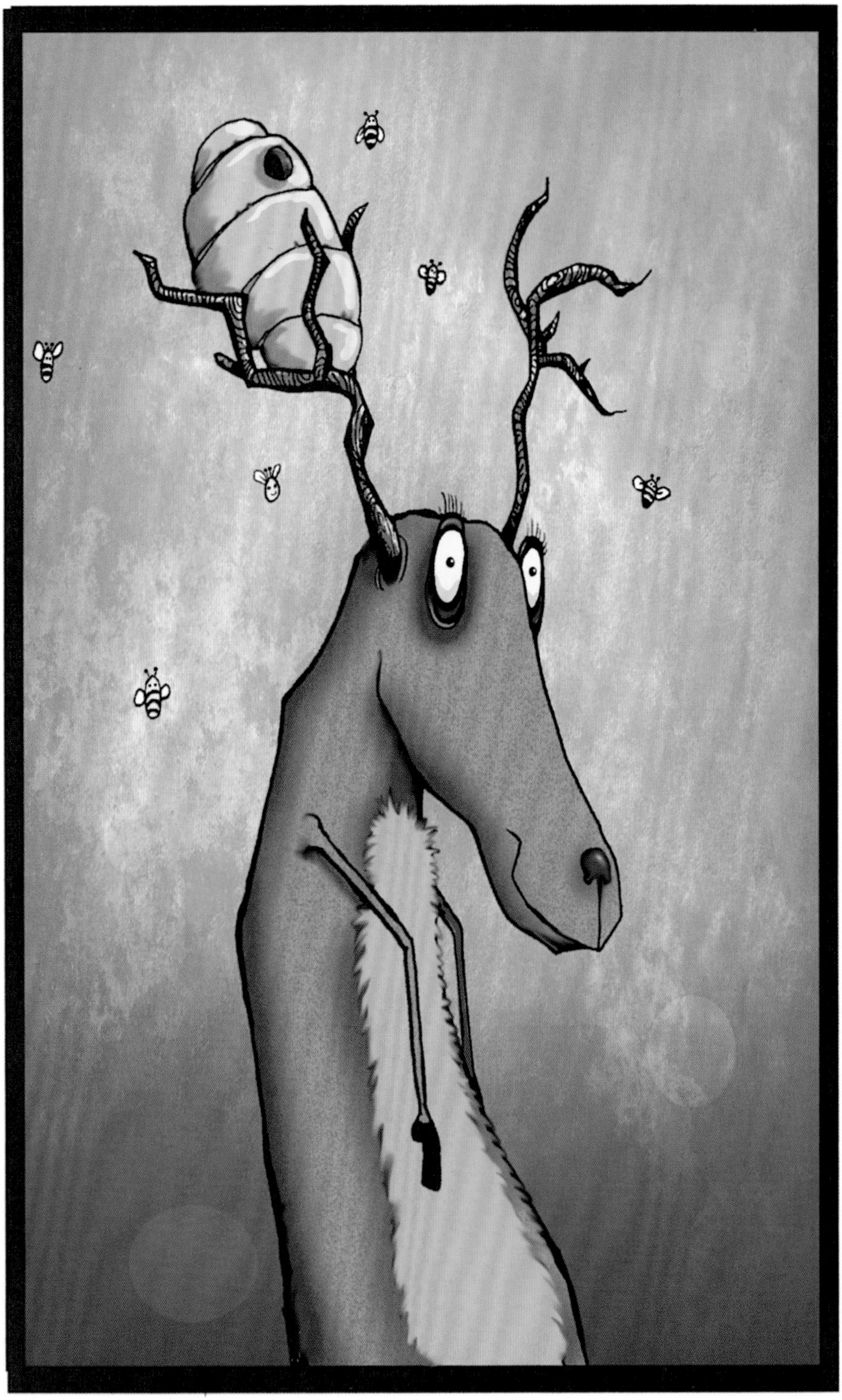

To consumate this love,
they decided to kiss.
Unfortunately for them,
the bee did miss.
An accidental sting ripped out
what the bee had inside.
Without her innards,
she shortly there died.

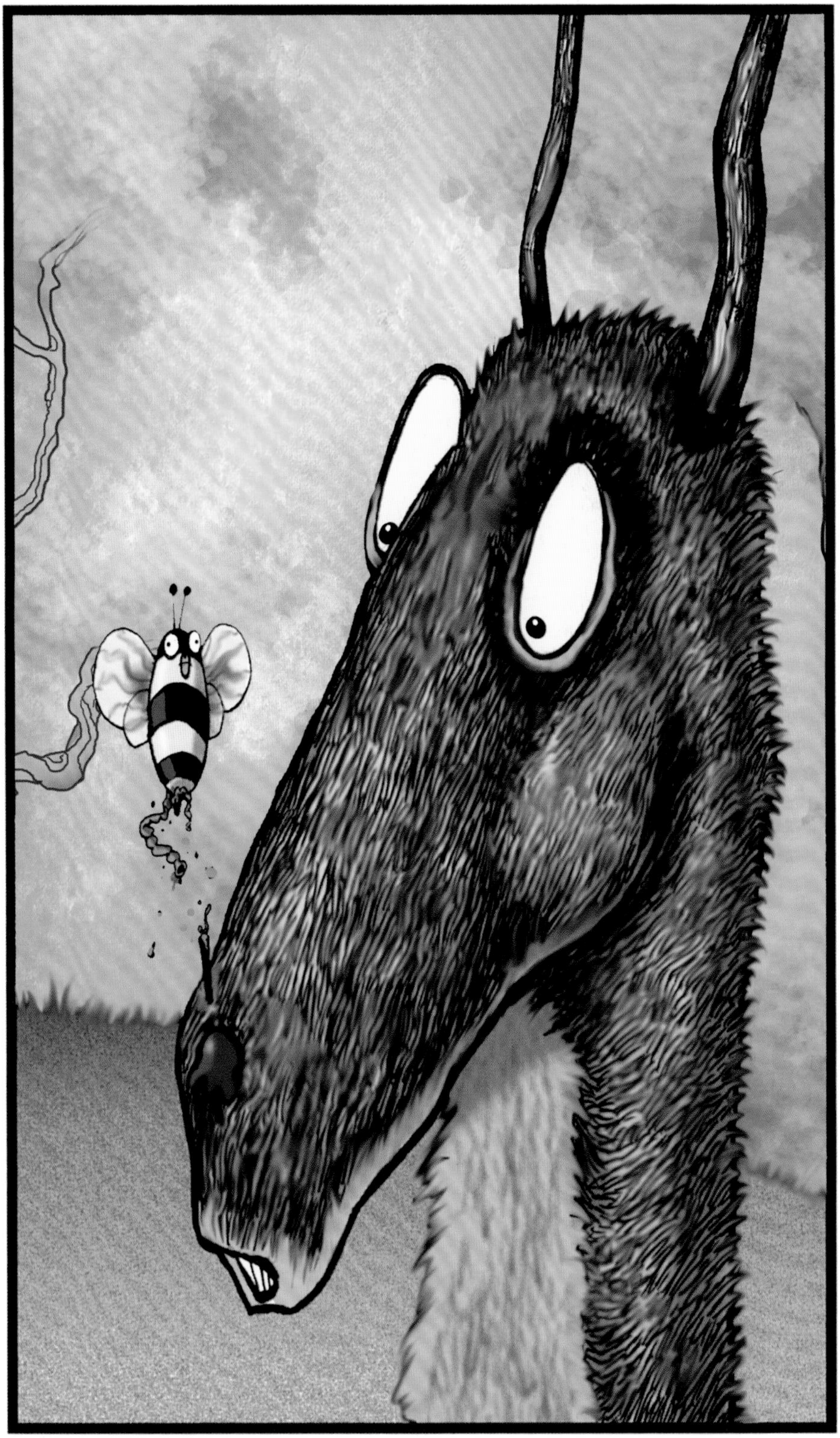

Stricken with grief,
the reindeer then sobbed.
Devastated,
his heart had been robbed.
Sadly
this was not to be the worst of things.
It turned out
he was allergic to bee stings.

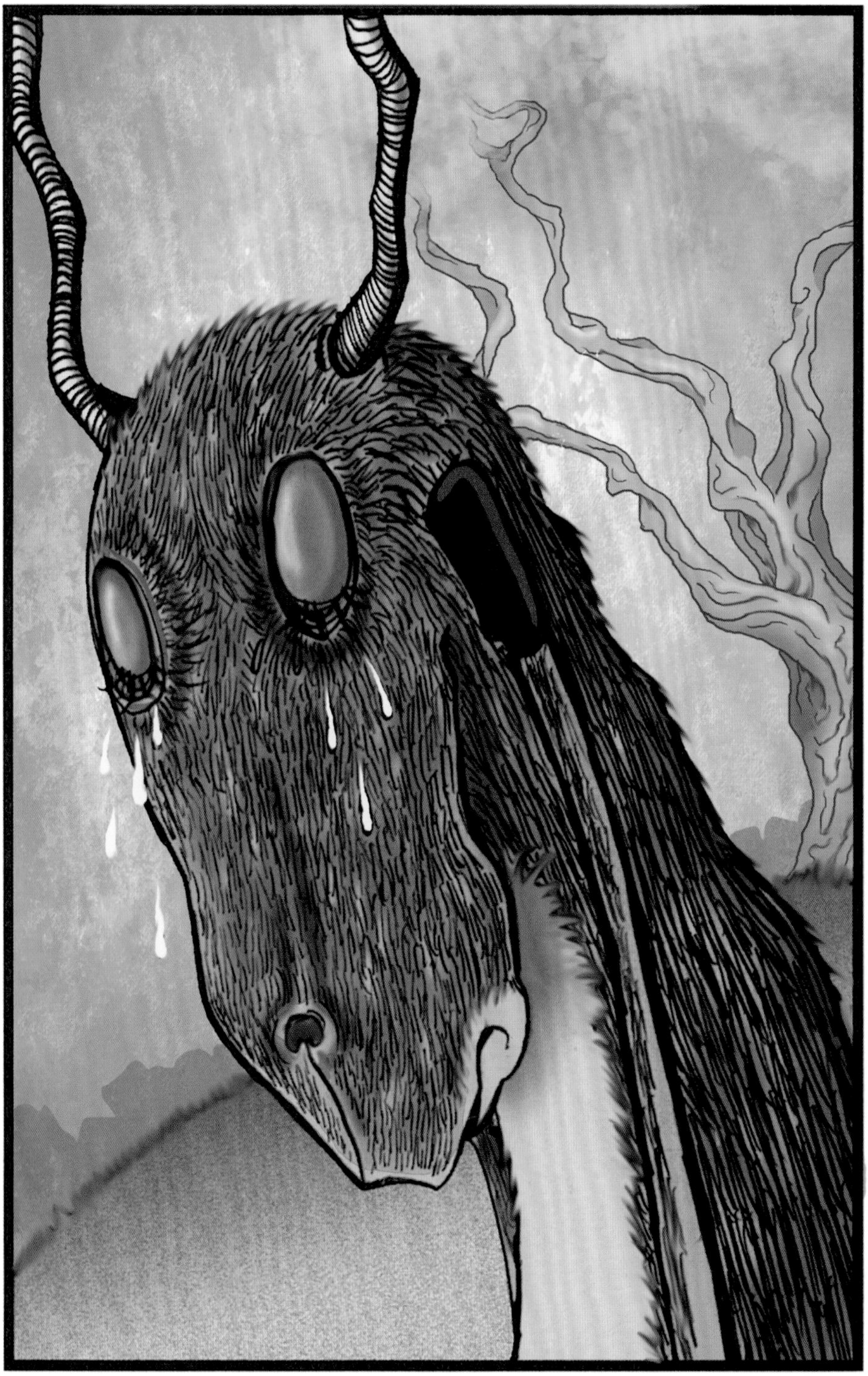

Clutching his chest,
he let out his final breath,
turned a strange colour...
then succumbed to death.
The awkward day came –
no one knew what to do.
The proceedings were silent
as they buried the two.

WEIRD FAMILY WEIRD BABY

It's not a question
of maybe –
A weird family
makes a weird baby.

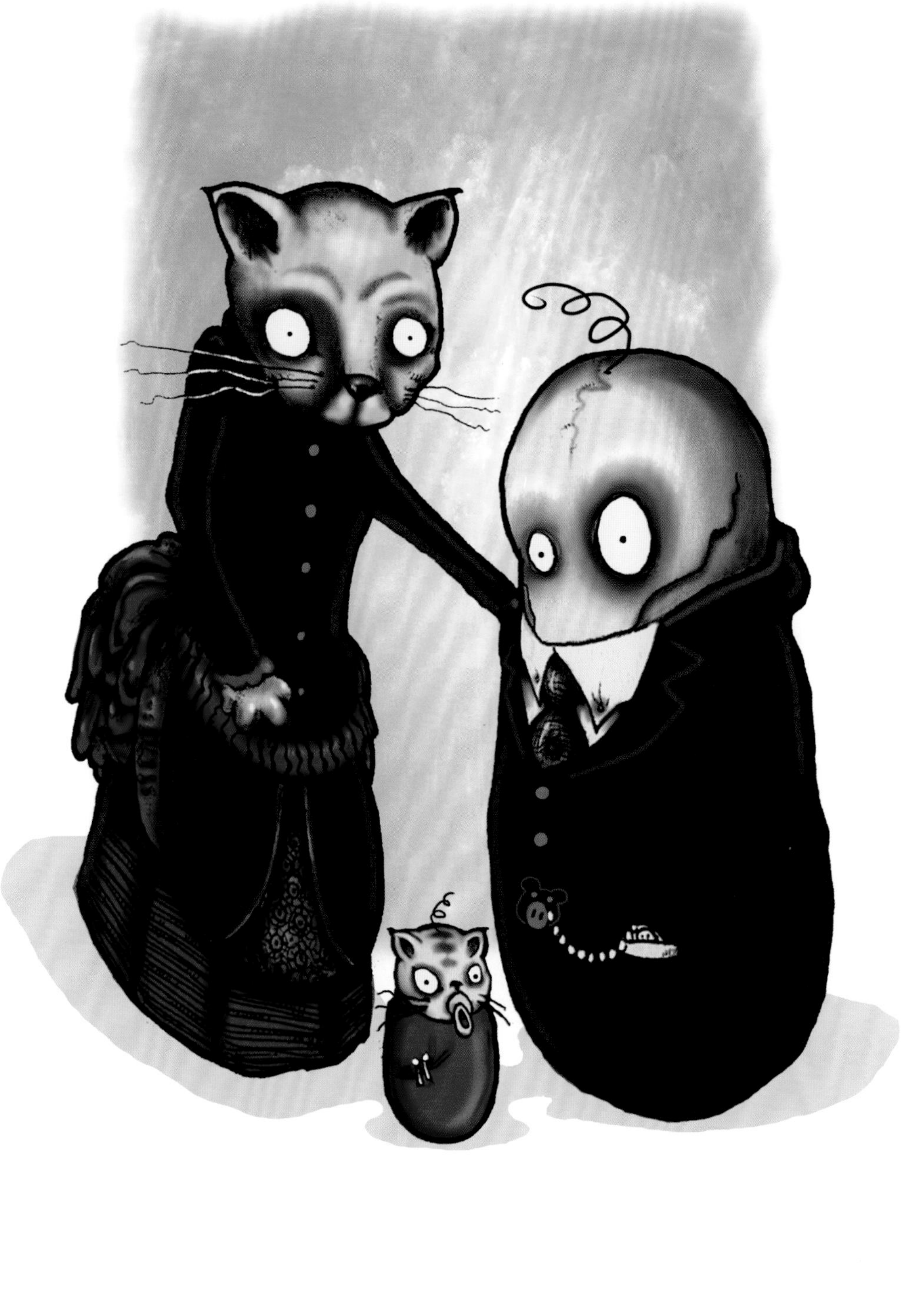

FLY PAPER

A pleasant scent
beckoned me,
but I didn't know
it was so sticky.
I just cannot
fly or get free,
so now misery loves
a little company.

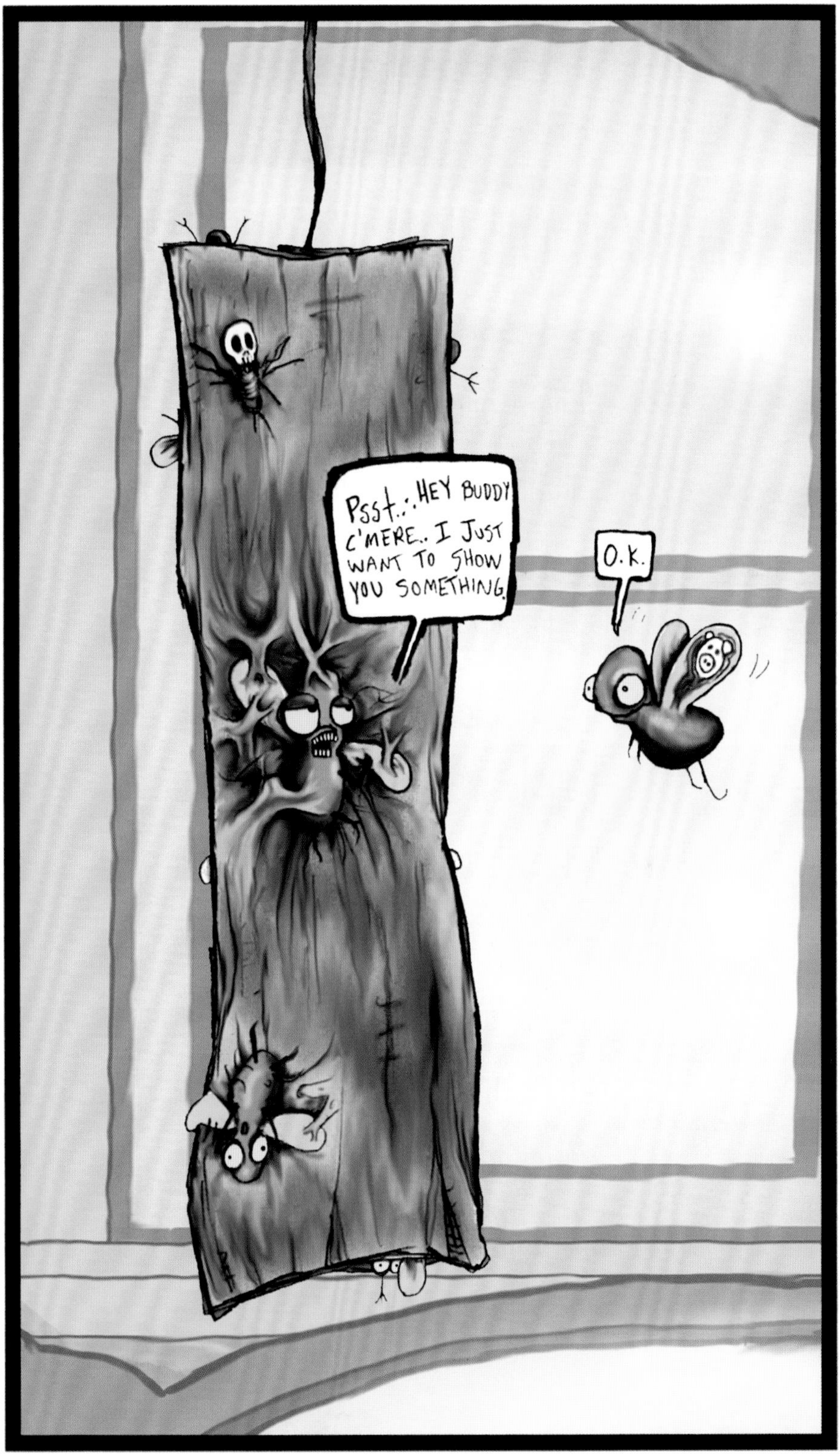
Psst..:.HEY BUDDY C'MERE.. I JUST WANT TO SHOW YOU SOMETHING.
O.K.

DANCE OF THE BEDBUGS

There once was a bear
named Popple Fubbie.
He had a special pillow
that he called his "wubbie".
Late one nite,
Popple was very tired –
the thought of sleep
he admired.
So on went his jammies,
and he grabbed his bunny,
flicked on his light –
but something was funny.

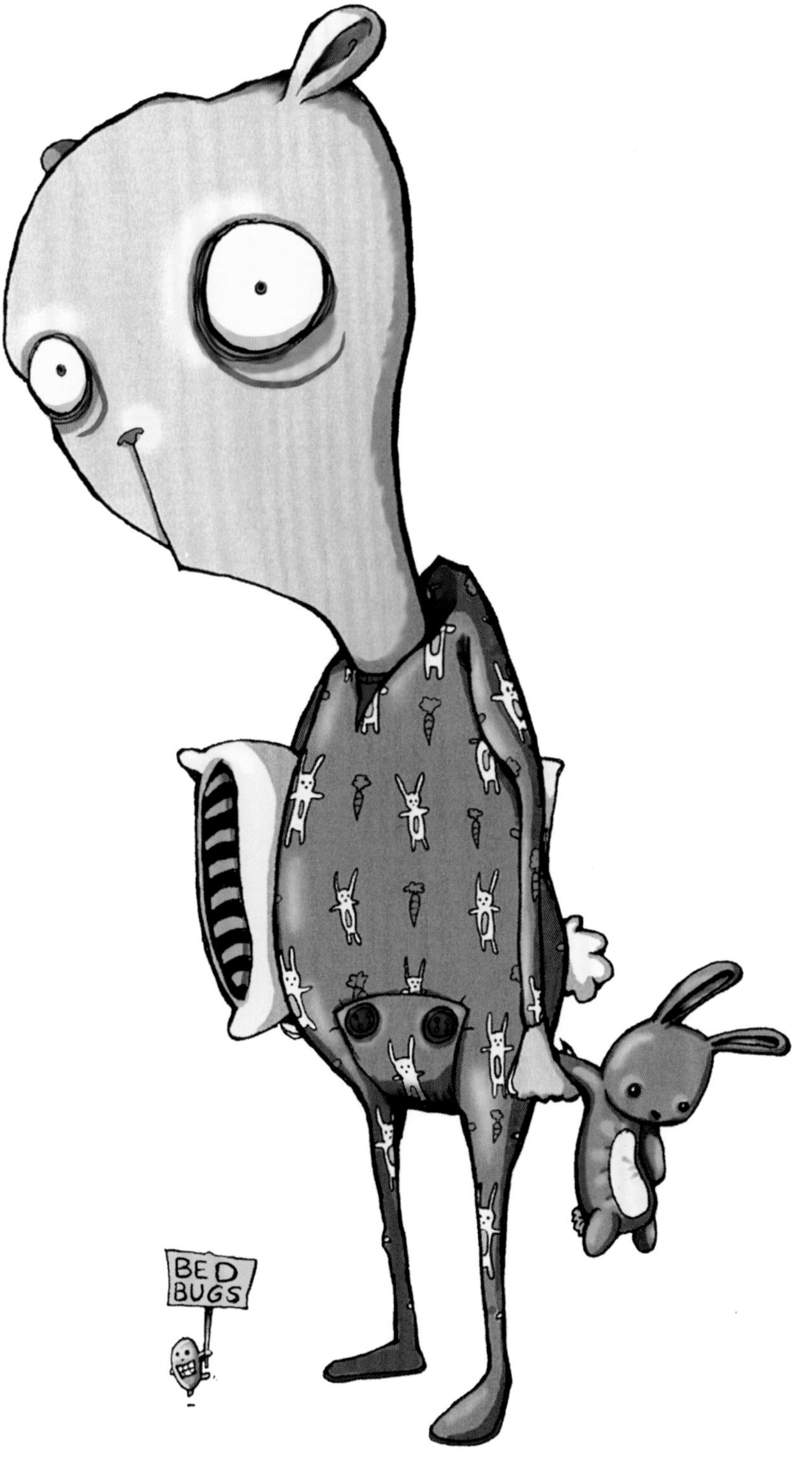
BED
BUGS

A dozen tiny bugs
danced on his bed.
Happy to see him –
bedbugs to be fed.
"Oh no!," exclaimed Popple.
"I can't sleep here.
You bugs eating me,
I surely do fear."
Looking around at all the bugs
in their places,
a thought of fear
could be seen on all their faces.
As Popple turned to leave,
in his bed he would not be sleeping.
He heard a weird sound –
a baby bedbug was weeping.

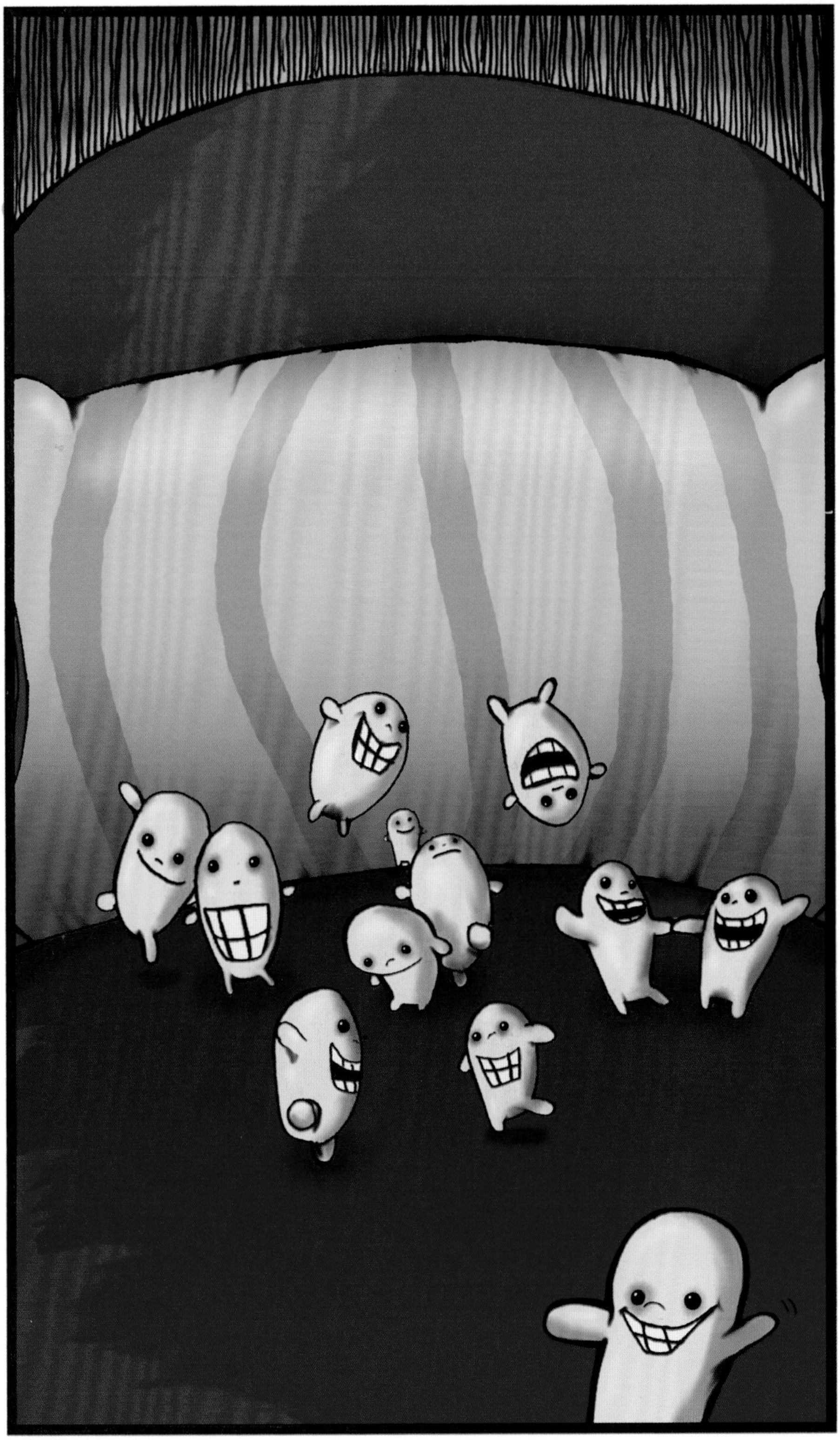

"Why do you cry,
tiny bug on my sheets?"
"I don't want to starve,"
said the bug.
"You were my only eats."
"I'm really sorry little bug
if it seems selfish of me –
but if you eat me,
I will no longer be
alive to do all the things that I please."
"We beg you," cried the bugs,
now sadly on their knees.
"I'll just sleep in another room,"
and away turned the bear.
"Oh, after you're sleeping,
we'll just eat you in there."

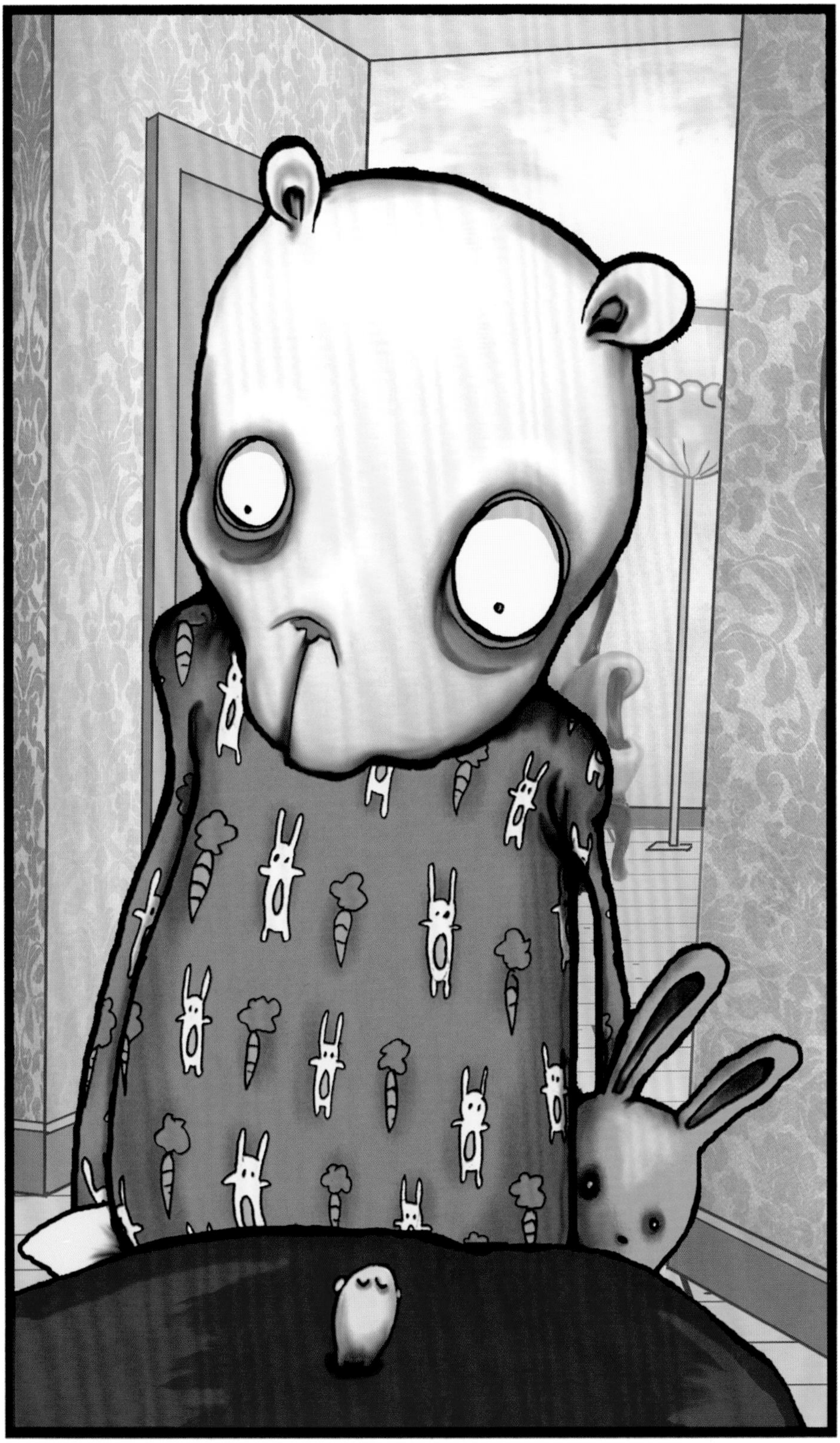

Suddenly Popple realized
the trouble he was in.
He couldn't go to sleep
without becoming din-din.
He played lots of loud music
and coffee he drank,
but slowly into
subconsciousness he sank.
Popple held his eyes open –
his life he must keep.
The bedbugs began yawning,
trying to trick him to sleep.
He fought as long as he could
before he began to topple –
but in the end,
the bugs had a bowl full of Popple.

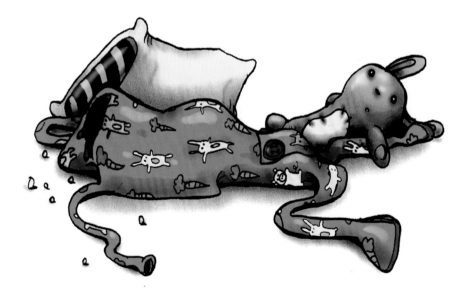

BOODINI AND CHOOBIE

Boodini and Choobie -
what a magical pair.
A rotting magician...
a decomposing hare...
a trick gone wrong...
an illusion gone awry....
Their very last trick
was refusing to die.

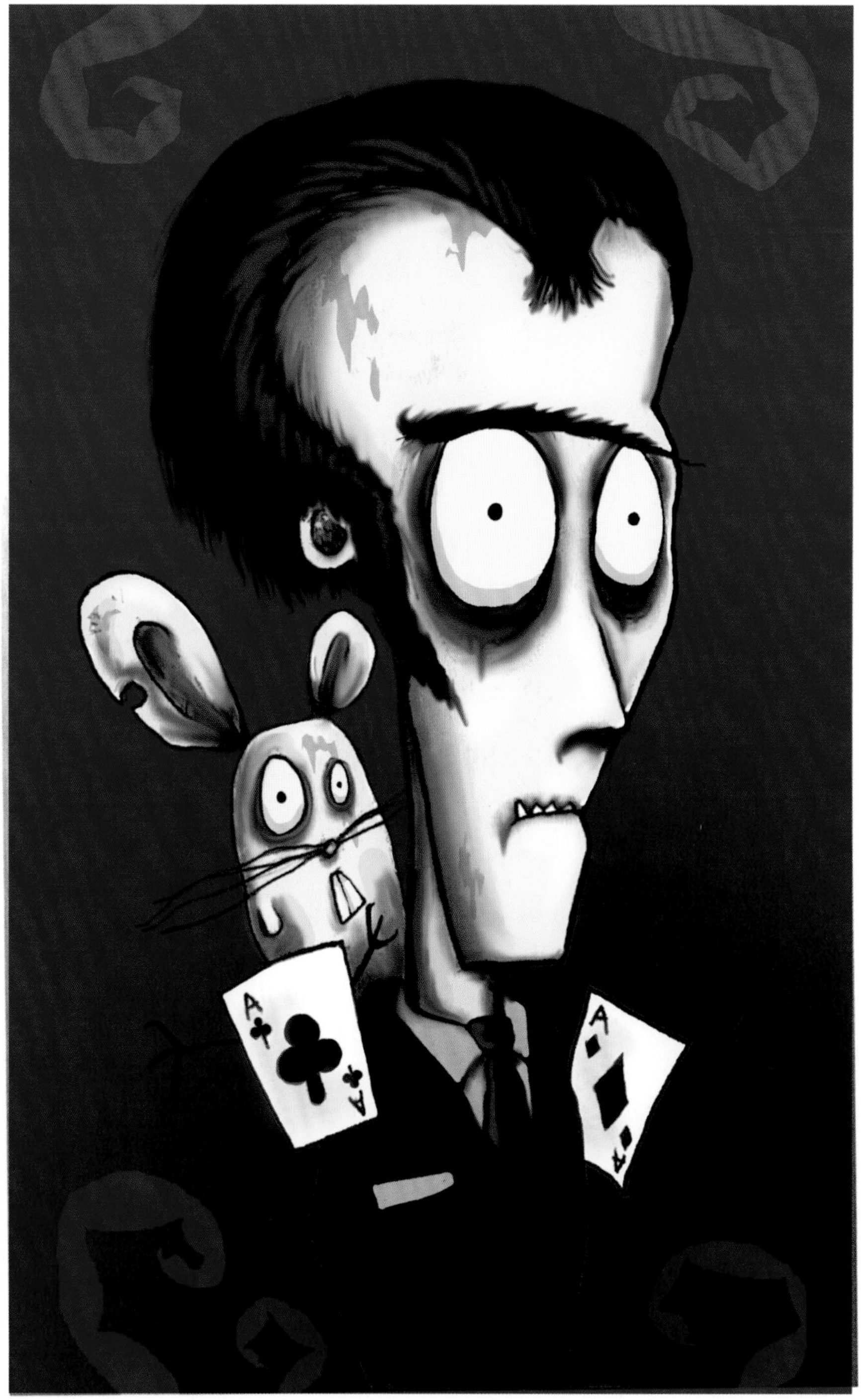

THE GUY WITH A THING ON HIS HEAD

There's not a whole lot
that can be said
for the poor guy
with a thing on his head.

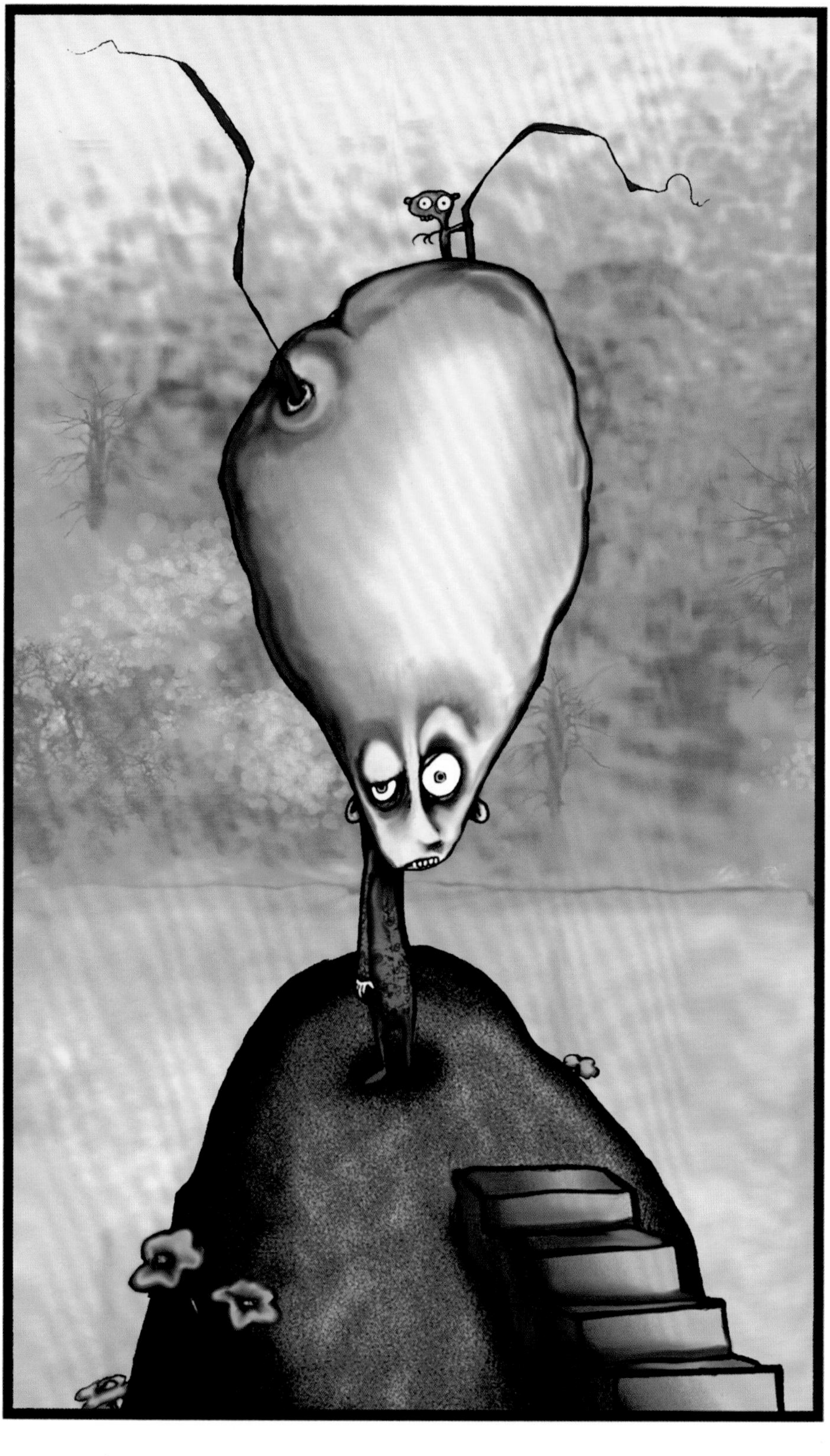

EDDIE POE

Long ago
lived Eddie Poe,
in love with pumpkins
more than he should be.
Everyday he would visit.
If not, he would miss it.
Eddie would be a pumpkin
if he could be.

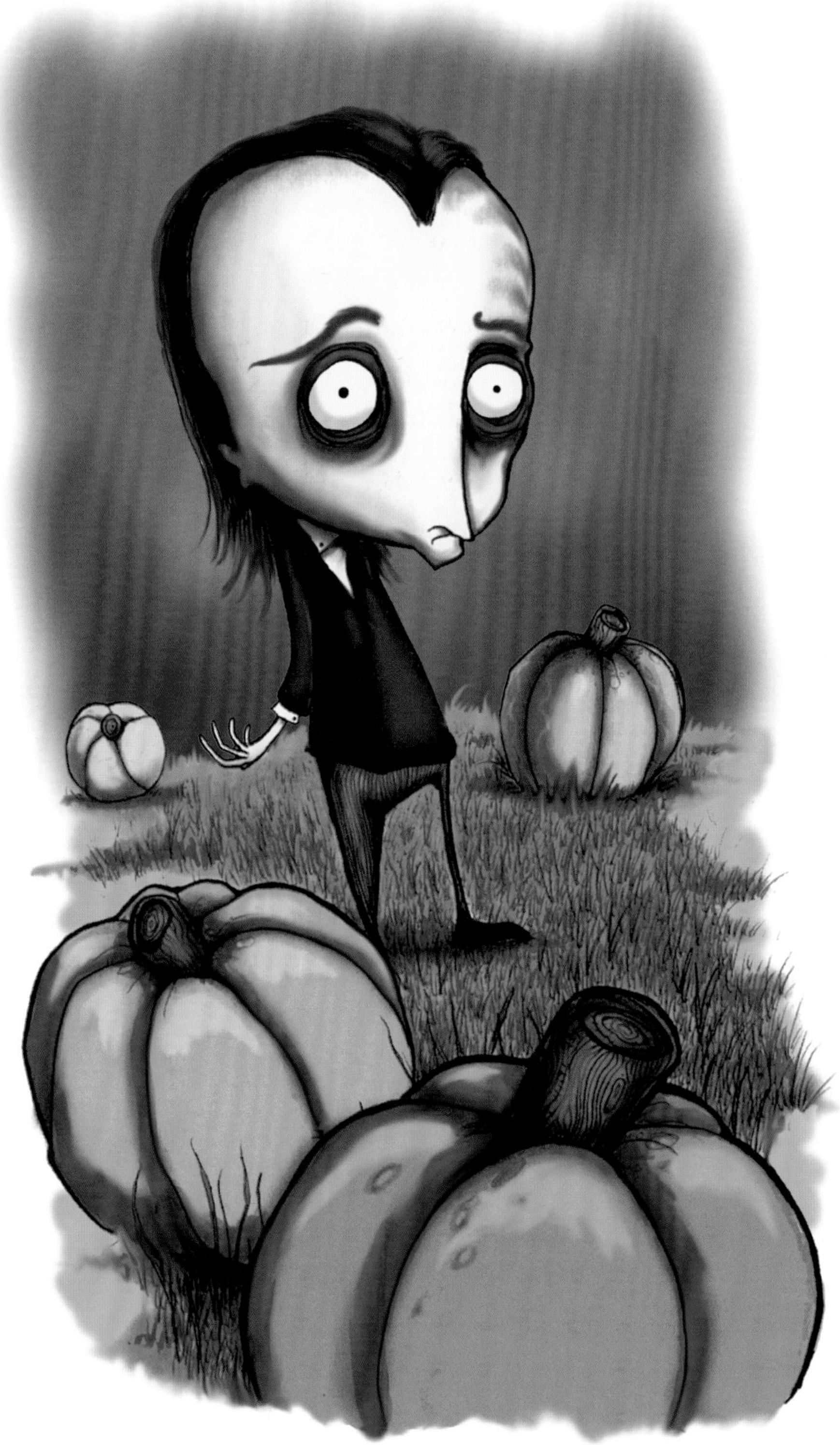

He didn't go away.
Instead he did stay
and fell asleep
in the pumpkin patch.
When he awoke,
nature played a joke.
Now he and pumpkins
did match.

Someone took him
that day
who loved pumpkins
in a different way –
and made him into a yummy pie.
After this you see
you have to agree
what a horrible way for Eddie to die.

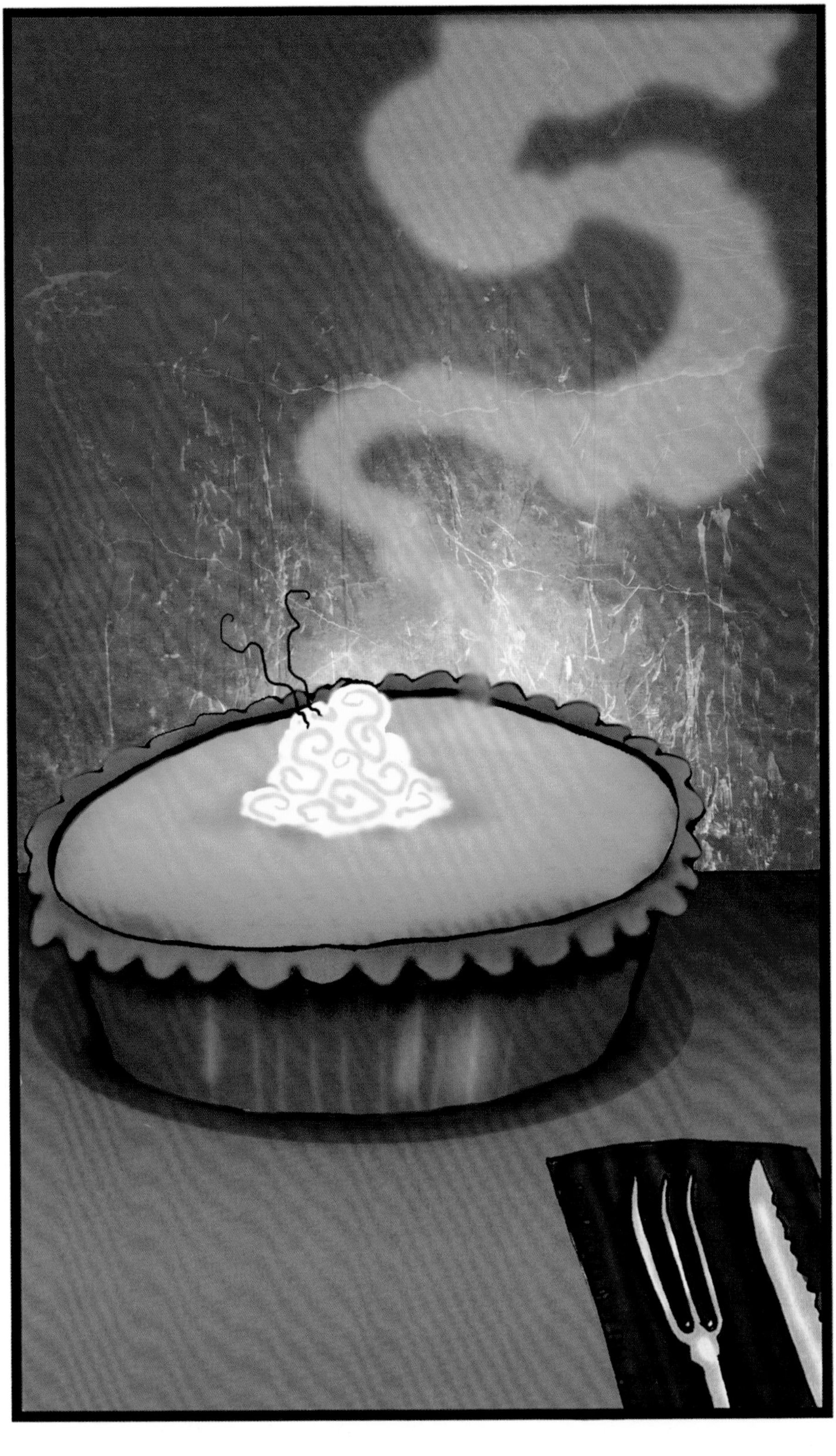

Hey!

Guess what boys and girls!

Many drawings in this book have little piggies hidden somewhere among them.

Why? I don't know.

I also don't think that this shirt is funny.

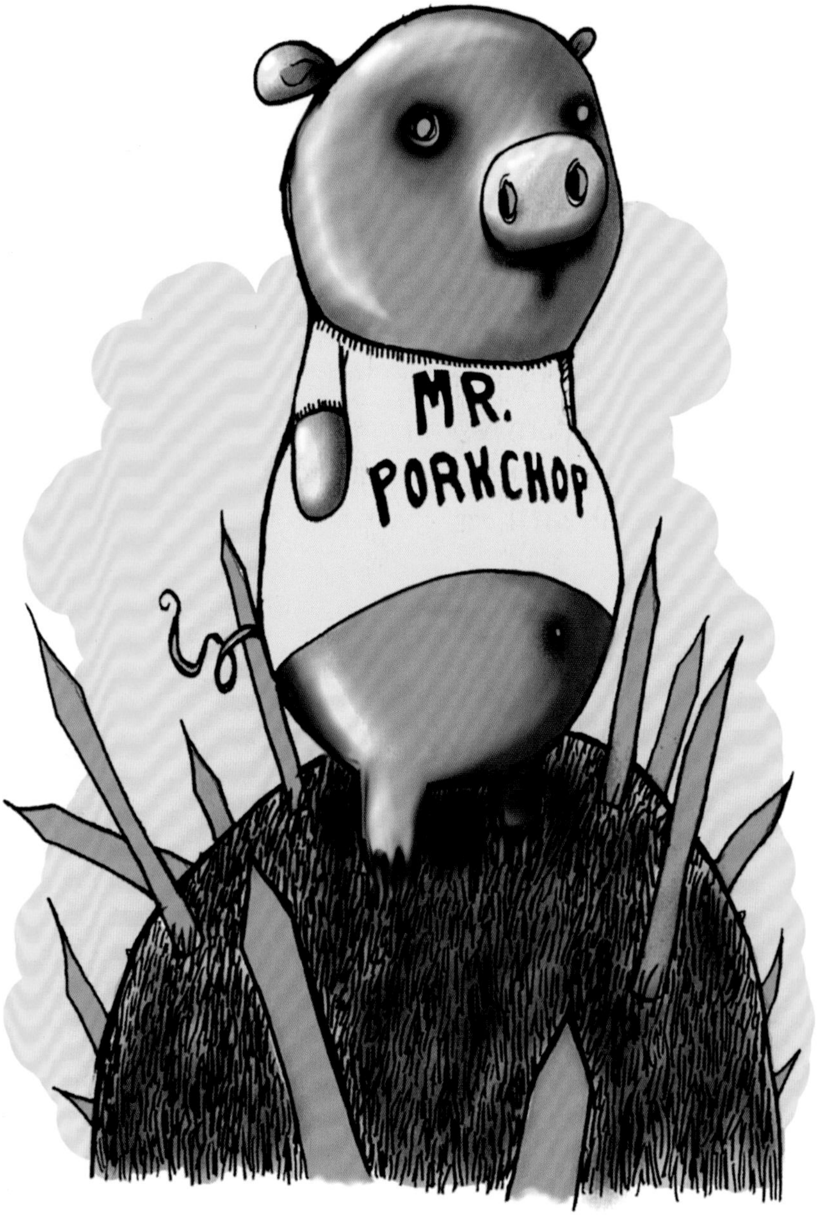
MR. PORKCHOP

ABOUT THE AUTHOR

An illustrator for numerous "underground" magazines, Roman Dirge created his best known character, Lenore in 1992. The adventures of the cute little dead girl were seen in mini-comics and various magazines for several years afterward.

After running into Tim Burton at Soloman's garage in Los Angeles, Roman showed him his artwork. Mr. Burton described his style as "beautiful" and "timeless".

This was encouraging.

After toying around working as a magician and a make up artist for several years, Roman decided to take the plunge and do "Lenore" as a full comic book series. "Lenore" became an instant cult success and launched Roman into other artistic endeavours such as character design for TV animation and illustrating children's books. Currently, Roman resides in California where he loves tattoos, video games, martial arts, magic tricks and writing about himself in the third person.

THE CAT WITH A REALLY BIG HEAD

THE STORY OF A CAT CALLED CAT AND HIS STUPIDLY RIDICULOUS BIG HEAD!

From the twisted imagination of Roman Dirge, the Michelangelo of the macabre, comes his latest gothic masterpiece, a collection of two of his strangest and weirdest tales that will take you from the bottom of a cat bowl to the heart of human despair. Featuring revised art and new coloring by Adam Bolton.

www.titan-comics.com

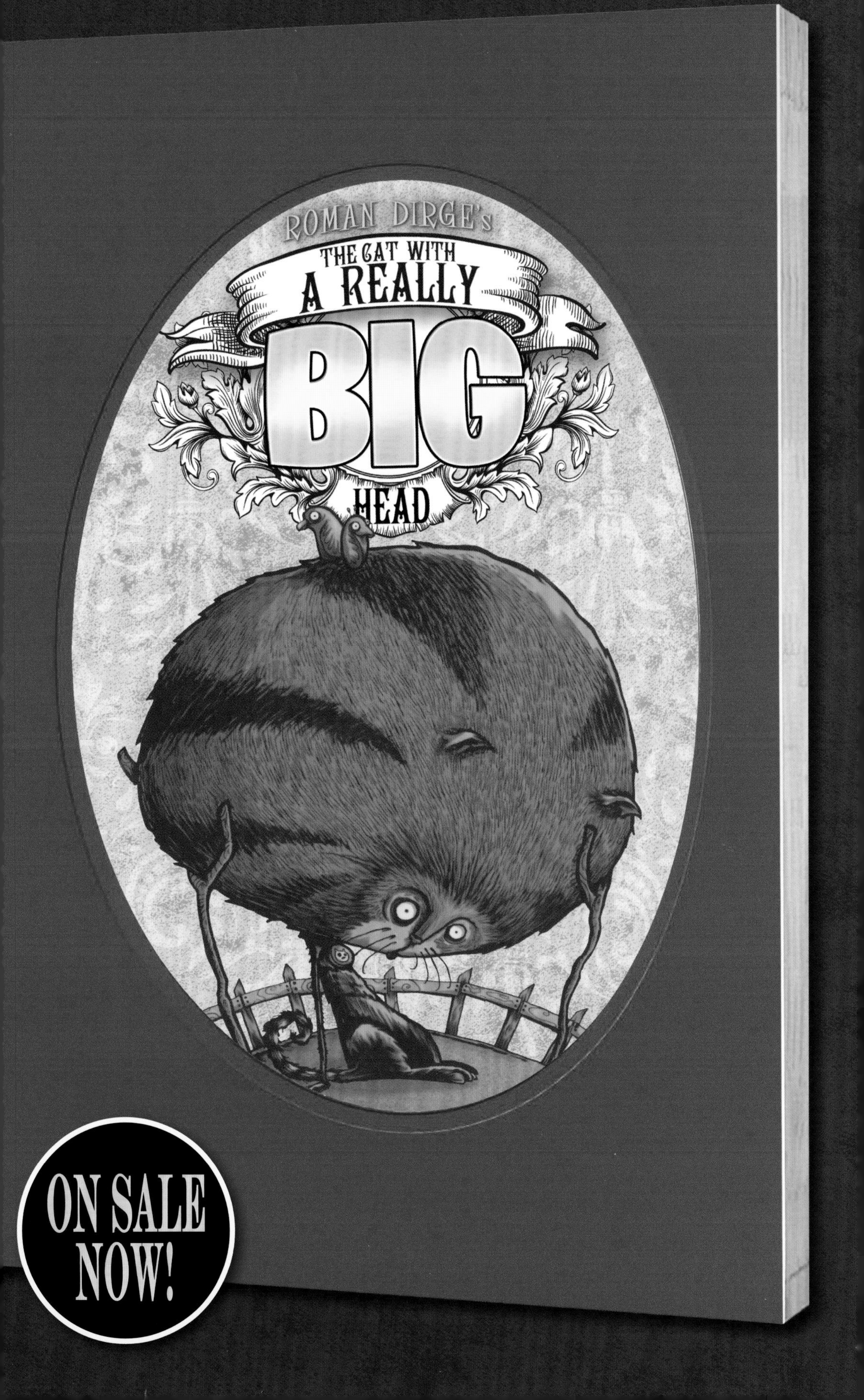
ROMAN DIRGE's
THE CAT WITH
A REALLY
BIG
HEAD
ON SALE
NOW!

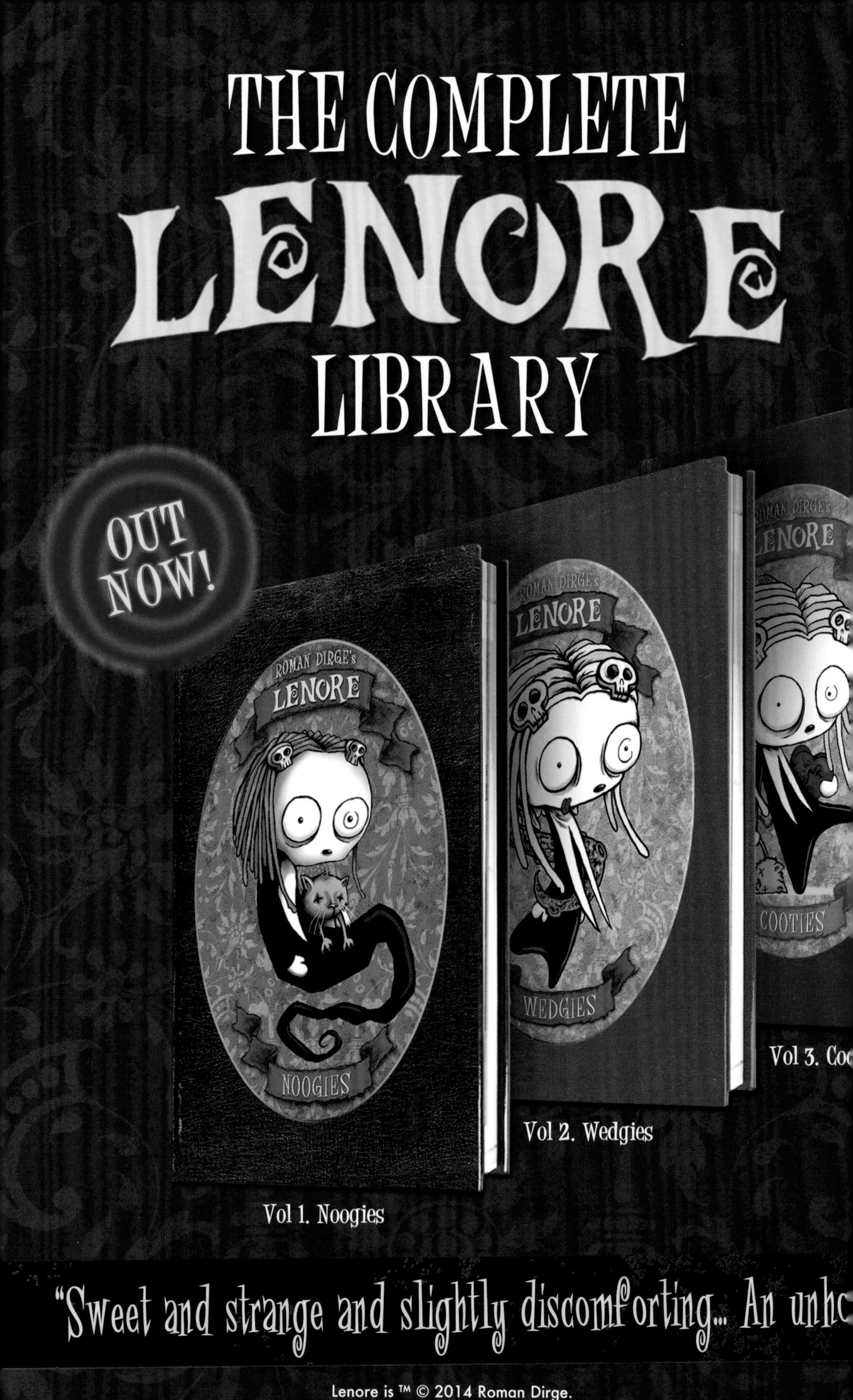
THE COMPLETE
LENORE
LIBRARY
OUT NOW!
ROMAN DIRGE's
LENORE
NOOGIES
WEDGIES
COOTIES
Vol 1. Noogies
Vol 2. Wedgies
"Sweet and strange and slightly discomforting... An unhc

Featuring digitally re-mastered artwork
in full-color and packed with bonus art,
pin-ups, guest art, comic strips
and extras!

Vol 6. Pink Bellies

Vol 5. Purple Nurples

Vol 4. Swirlies

COLLECT THE WHOLE HELLISHLY HORRIFIC AND HORRIBLE SAGA.

on between Tim Burton and Dr. Seuss." - Los Angeles Times

www.titan-comics.com

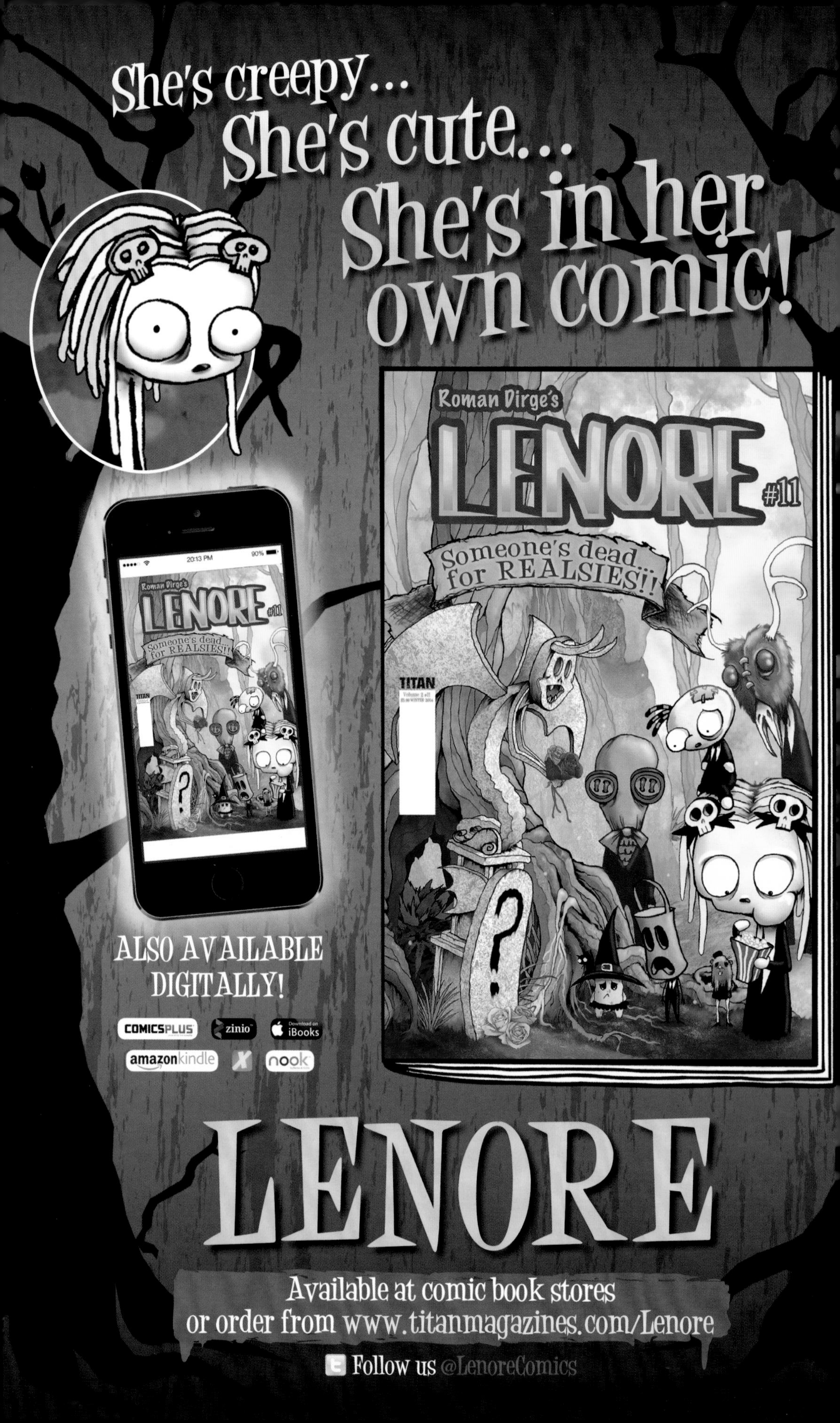

She's creepy...
She's cute...
She's in her own comic!
Roman Dirge's
LENORE #11
Someone's dead for REALSIES!!
TITAN
ALSO AVAILABLE DIGITALLY!
COMICSPLUS
zinio
iBooks
amazonkindle
nook
LENORE
Available at comic book stores
or order from www.titanmagazines.com/Lenore
Follow us @LenoreComics